"There are thousands of books on communications—this one stands out! THE REVOLUTIONARY COMMUNICATOR is a new approach with new insights, and it is practical. It will make you a better communicator, while giving you a dramatic view of the greatest communicator of all."
—**BERT DECKER,** best-selling author, founder of communications training company Decker Communications, and communications commentator for the NBC *TODAY Show*

"The Gospels make it clear that huge crowds listened to Jesus with rapt attention. Jesus was a communicator without equal. Medefind and Lokkesmoe insightfully explain the principles at the heart of Jesus' skill in a practical way. At the same time, they remind the reader of his redemptive spirituality that goes far beyond mere technique."
—**CHUCK COLSON,** author, speaker, and founder of Break Point, a national radio commentary

"I've consulted at The White House, in boardrooms, at business schools and CEO boot camps, from Capitol Hill to Silicon Valley. THE REVOLUTIONARY COMMUNICATOR will take you to a higher level—both as a speaker and as a human. It unearths lost treasures to great communication."
—**TIM KOEGEL**, presentation and media training coach, author of *The Exceptional Presenter*

"This book captures in words what is so missing in our media-driven world. Through principles accessible to anyone, our communication can build the depth and closeness we desire but rarely find. Whether in quiet moments with my daughter or addressing a political convention, these truths create meaningful connection and lasting influence."
—**SHARON RUNNER,** Assemblywoman, California's 36th District

"THE REVOLUTIONARY COMMUNICATOR challenges us to become listeners, questioners, and storytellers, the better to make true, deep connections with the people in our world. A simple yet radical book."
—**JANET BATCHLER,** Hollywood instructor and screenwriter who, with her husband, wrote the international blockbuster film *Batman Forever*

"Medefind and Lokkesmoe offer a unique and compelling perspective on communication, taking us beyond the superficial mantras of tacticians and strategists to explore the deeper meaning of human interaction. Through the clever juxtaposition of examples from the life of Christ, our own everyday experiences, historical events, and the familiar worlds of fiction, these authors identify the roots of real communication: truth and charity. This work, both literary and meditative, will appeal to readers of all backgrounds and interests. The insights these authors share with us will enrich our understanding as well as our prayer."
—**DR. PATRICIA PHALEN,** Director of Graduate Studies, School of Media and Public Affairs, The George Washington University

"Medefind and Lokkesmoe offer practical observations and suggestions that could benefit marriages, movies, meetings, and mega-churches. They have filled their book with anecdotes and examples—any number of which would make some pretty good movies or TV shows—and explain how to incorporate Jesus' style of communication into everyday life. In this age of media saturation, it is fascinating to be reminded that, thousands of years ago, one man in Jerusalem modeled the best way to hear and be heard. And he did it without a mic or a modem."
—**DEAN BATALI,** Co-Executive Producer, *That '70s Show*

"As a quarterback, congressman, and now businessman, I've seen again and again that communicating well is critical to success. THE REVOLUTIONARY COMMUNICATOR takes a refreshing look at the greatest teacher and communicator ever, and offers principles that can make a tremendous difference in business, leadership, and personal relations. Simple, powerful insights are here for all to understand."
—**THE HONORABLE J.C. WATTS,** former member of Congress and professional football player

"This book is important. THE REVOLUTIONARY COMMUNICATOR unpacks central characteristics of the way Christ made his message real in the lives of those who heard it. It can help people from all walks of life become better communicators and gain a glimpse into the mechanics of living out God's reign in the midst of daily life."
—**JASON A. EVANS,** Senior editor of Next-Wave.org

THE
REVOLUTIONARY
COMMUNICATOR

THE

REVOLUTIONARY
COMMUNICATOR

SEVEN PRINCIPLES JESUS LIVED TO
IMPACT, CONNECT AND LEAD

JEDD
MEDEFIND

ERIK
LOKKESMOE

[RELEVANTBOOKS]

Published by Relevant Books
A division of Relevant Media Group, Inc.

www.relevantbooks.com
www.relevantmediagroup.com

© 2004 by Relevant Media Group

Design: Relevant Solutions
www.relevant-solutions.com

Cover design by Joshua Smith, Jeremy Kennedy
Interior design by Jeremy Kennedy

Relevant Books is a registered trademark of Relevant Media Group, Inc.,
and is registered in the U.S. Patent and Trademark Office.

For information or bulk orders:
RELEVANT MEDIA GROUP, INC.
POST OFFICE BOX 951127
LAKE MARY, FL 32795
407-333-7152

Library of Congress Control Number: 2004094215
International Standard Book Number: 0-9746942-5-8

04 05 06 07 9 8 7 6 5 4 3 2 1

Printed in the United States of America

Jedd

To the courageous women whose gifts make me who I am.
My wife, Rachel—best friend and lover, true companion,
loyal champion, and the inspiration to pursue that
of which I now only dream.
My mother, Colleen—who poured her life into me as I grew,
and continues to give me strength through her wisdom,
example, and love.

Erik

To my wife, Monica, who communicates
love in the way she lives.

Solo Deo Gloria

ACKNOWLEDGMENTS

For aid and advice along the journey of this book, the authors would like to thank Janet Batchler, Karen Berger, Aerin Bryant, Bill Coombe, Sean Dimond, Ken Germer, Dr. Mike Giuliano, Casey Hall, Jason Hamm, Rev. Glenn Hoburg, Jared and Jody Jones, Larry and Marsha Jones, Danny and Emily Kapic, Randy Kemp, Tim Koegel, Matt and Summer Kronberg, Tim and Patti Lokkesmoe, Bob Massey, Dr. Jon McNeff, Maynard and Colleen Medefind, Helen Jean Medefind, Grace Metzger, Krista Obitts, Chris Perrin, Mike and Brittney Peterson, Dr. Pat Phalen, Betty Scalice, Joseph Scalice, Roger and Janet Scalice, Trey and Kristina Sklar, Rev. Jim Tonkowich, Jim Troyer, Dr. Gary and Marlene Van Brocklin, and Tim Washer.

And a unique and special thanks to Dr. Greg Spencer, who not only helped to birth and shape many of the ideas contained in this book, but also embodies them as a teacher, husband, father, and friend.

"What do you have that you were not given?"

TABLE OF CONTENTS

PREFACE

The award-winning film *Lost in Translation* offered a haunting reflection of modern life and relationship. In the dizzying world of downtown Tokyo, two Americans—a neglected young wife and an aging movie star—strike up an unlikely friendship. Around them, city lights glitter, and technology dazzles. Manicured gardens and high-rise restaurants call for exploration, while eager hosts offer nonstop entertainment.

Yet even while feasting on this rich faire, the two visitors are left empty. Absent from virtually every human interaction is any real sense of shared understanding or connection. All that communication is supposed to provide remains missing, apparently lost in translation.

Critics showered the film with praise, recognizing in it the world most of us inhabit, at least in part. It is a world flooded with images, information, and interaction ... yet still somehow vaguely disappointing. Although wired for every connection imaginable, there remains lingering over all a troubling sense of disconnectedness. Even personal conversations often feel thin and insubstantial, offering hardly more sustenance than the gruel fed to Oliver Twist. We eat, but remain hungry; exchange information, but experience little of lasting value.

Dare we seek more from communication in a media age?

Is it worth our effort to seek friendships that are fuller and more intimate? Should we bother to wish for authentic connection between our spiritual values and the workaday realities of sales reports, oil changes, and cranky children? Can we go beyond information exchange to influence lives and leave lasting impact upon our community?

This book is built upon the conviction that the way we communicate can create more—both for ourselves and for our culture.

For both of us authors, communication is the centerpiece of our professions. Erik has filled numerous press secretary and speechwriter positions within Washington, D.C.'s "beltway," and now runs the communications for a federal agency. Jedd's post is three thousand miles away, serving as a chief of staff in the Legislature of the nation's most populous state. Each day brings a jumble of press conferences and speeches, editorials and articles, focus groups and polling data. Our job is to mold the message, cut through the noise, shape opinions ... and hope it sticks.

Amid this wearying pursuit of crisp words and vibrant delivery, we have come to a new and profound respect for the way of communication lived out by a figure we had never really thought of as a communicator, Jesus of Nazareth. Yet the deeper we look, the more we are impressed. Indeed, he invites nothing less than revolution at the heart of communication in a media age.

Both of us have held deep faith in Jesus for many years. Even so, it has been disturbing—and also marvelously bracing—to encounter Jesus' skill in a realm we once considered our territory. Our lives, quite literally, will never be the same.

However, let us be clear from the beginning—in writing a book about communication, we do not wish to pose as master communicators, nor do we intend merely to share from our own skills and knowledge. Rather, we desire to unearth together the profound communication truths lived by Jesus and displayed throughout history in others whose communication became great as they responded to his lead.

These truths, no doubt, will leave some surprised. They are subversive, challenging prevailing assumptions about communication, just as Jesus scandalized the unquestioned notions of his own day.

But in an age exhausted by spin, hype, and image, we are convinced Jesus' approach to communication offers an irresistible opportunity to connect with those around us at the deepest levels, and to draw them to what is higher, fuller, and more enduring. Why would we settle for anything less?

Jedd Medefind, Sacramento, CA
Erik Lokkesmoe, Washington, D.C.
2004

"There are two kinds of revolutionists, as of most things—a good kind and a bad. The bad revolutionists destroy conventions by appealing to fads —fashions that are newer than conventions. The good do it by appealing to facts that are older than conventions."

—G.K. Chesterton

INTRODUCTION
Who He Was and What He Said

He was born to a teen mother in a cattle shed on the outskirts of a backwater village. Goats and sheep and hens surrounded his makeshift crib, constructed quickly from brittle hay and an old blanket pungent with donkey sweat.

From all appearances, this baby wasn't going to amount to much.

At an early age, his father taught him to work with his hands. Some say he was a woodworker, handy with the chisel and saw, repairing old tables and crafting new chairs. Others speculate that he built with stone, traveling three miles every morning to job sites in the Roman city of Sephoris.

Whatever the tasks, tradition recounts that his callused hands produced quality work, accepted with little thought by neighbors and friends. To them, he was simply another Nazarene, a carpenter's son—as common as the materials with which he built.

Yet in just three tumultuous years, this Jewish tradesman split history in two.

He shattered the status quo like faux jewelry, leaving the elitists who'd been selling it trembling with rage. He celebrated life with rebels and dined with outcasts. His words echoed over mountainsides and desert footpaths, spreading like a prairie wildfire among illiterate townsfolk and dignitaries alike, resounding in palace halls, crowded marketplaces, and marble-walled temples.

Everywhere he ventured, crowds pressed in, eager to hear anything this teller of stories had to say. They strained to touch his clothes, moved back when he did something unexpected, like etching in the sand or spitting in the mud. For days on end, multitudes stood listening to his words, transfixed. Tax cheats and call girls gave up their dubious occupations to be near him, and fishmongers abandoned their boats. Riots and rumors dogged his path. In his presence, the influential and best-dressed felt threatened, even terrified. The masses adored him.

Who was this nobody turned notable?

They called him Jesus. He's a divisive figure, no question. Much good and much evil has been done in his name. He claimed to be the Son of God, the Savior, a Shepherd to the lost and blind. Witnesses attest that he performed miracles, even raised the dead. He described himself as the way, the truth, and the life. Even skeptics find him enthralling. It is no exaggeration to say that he is the most studied, debated, and examined figure in all of history.

Napoleon Bonaparte, hardly known for being impressed with anyone but himself, voiced the thoughts of countless others in stating, "Everything in Christ astonishes me. His spirit overawes me, and his will confounds me. Between him and whoever else in the world, there is no possible term of comparison."[1]

Of course, it would be foolhardy to claim that Jesus' impact upon history flowed from his approach to communication alone. Without question, of far greater significance was the reality of who he was and what he said.

Even so, we must recognize the means by which this deeper reality was encountered. People experienced Jesus' person and message through his communication—in the words, questions, tools, and approach he chose to employ. To those who experienced Jesus, the medium was inseparable from the message. The way he communicated was itself a critical part of what he sought to convey.

And the results were astounding. Consider this: a tradesman with little formal education, never traveling more than a hundred miles from his place of birth, set in motion a movement that would continue for two thousand years in virtually every nation, every culture, and every language on earth.

A message first shared with a band of laborers and misfits, now reaches millions of people every year. The same stories are told over and over and over again, despite wars and famines and hurricanes and twenty-four-hour cable news and all the distractions that tend to leave reports out-dated even before they reach an audience.

And it all started without satellite dishes. Without the Internet. Without slick mailings or media campaigns. Without a college degree. Without talking points and teleprompters. Without press secretaries or the Gutenberg press. Without newspapers and newsletters. Without Tom Brokaw or MTV.

You see, the potency and effectiveness that marked Jesus' communication does not hinge upon money, position, or market-shares. Jesus had none of these things going for him. To discover the subtle secrets of Jesus' approach to communication, we must look elsewhere.

At its heart, Jesus' communication was not merely a set of honed skills or proficiencies. Rather, it drew its impact from deeper attributes of character and being. It is no different today. Effective communication is a way of living.

Of course, our world differs greatly from the one Jesus faced. Science and innovation have profoundly altered everyday life. Today's children routinely use media that would have left previous generations—not to mention the people of Jesus' day—gaping in wonder. Sounds and images invade nearly every moment, pursuing us and wooing us toward new products, ideas, and experiences. As one of California's top political consultants observed, lamenting his own inability to break through this static with even the most well-crafted advertising, "Our society is diseased with messages."

Yet despite all the technology, change, speed, and noise, the fundamental truths at the heart of powerful communication—the principles Jesus lived out in every communication act—have not changed at all.

Harnessing Jesus' communication truths does not require towering intellect or stature. An Ivy League degree or lengthy resumé are not prerequisites. These principles empower and enrich all who choose to employ them—whether journalist, homemaker, public official, or first grade teacher.

"I invent nothing. I rediscover," stated Auguste Rodin, sculptor of The Thinker and other stunning pieces. That is our quest as well, seeking to peel back presumptions of a media age and find again the radical communication modeled by Jesus. He practiced deep attentiveness (Chapter 1).He met people on their turf and in their terms (Chapter 2).He asked questions (Chapter 3).He offered himself with transparency (Chapter 4). He told stories (Chapter 5). He viewed time away from the crowd as more important than time in front of it (Chapter 6).He set his course by defining true communication success (Chapter 7).

The goal is as straightforward as it is formidable. Like young painters in the workshop of Da Vinci, we seek to become apprentices to this master communicator in an art of utmost importance to our lives: the way we communicate.

Jesus' approach was simple and uncomplicated. But don't mistake simple for unsophisticated. Living these communication truths, Jesus set in motion a revolution that continues to this day. And they remain as compelling today as ever. Ultimately, they have the power to subvert a culture of sound-bites and bull-horns, replacing it with a communication that goes further, deeper, longer, and wider than we can possibly imagine.

In a Media Age,
we assume that ...
In a sea of competing messages,
drawing attention to yourself
is the one essential.

In Every Age,
the truth is ...
Amid countless rival messages,
giving attention to others
in the one sure way to be heard.

CHAPTER ONE

ATTENTIVENESS:
Can You Hear Me Now?

Imagine a tuxedo-clad butler tip-toeing up to your seat along a heavy oak table. He lays before you a silver tray, its cover reflective as a mirror. "A gift from the master of the house," he states with a crisp English accent.

What waits underneath? Some dainty dish or culinary delight? Or could it be something else—a piece of jewelry or priceless artifact? You raise the lid gingerly, heart quickening with anticipation.

The only thing to greet your eyes, however, is the bottom of the tray. Empty space. You cast a disappointed glance toward the butler.

"Air," he explains smartly, "rich with oxygen."

Such a gift, of course, elicits little thankfulness under normal circumstances. But, were that same offering somehow presented to a sailor trapped beneath the waves, or a snowboarder buried by an avalanche, it would be a gift beyond value, making the Hope Diamond a worthless trinket in comparison. Such is the world in which we live. For whether or not we notice, most everyone around us bears the slight bluish tint of anoxia, a shortage of air. What is the oxygen for which they are starved? It is *attention*—the eager, caring eyes, ears, and hearts without which no human soul can flourish.

Technology has vastly expanded our ability to gaze out at the world. CNN and the Discovery Channel, web cams and chat rooms provide endless opportunities to amass information, probe distant realms, and gather details of others' lives. We prospect the globe with thoughtless finger flicks and button clicks.

But, as Randall Bush noted, this ease of learning and observation has not transformed us into "global villagers" nearly as much as some had predicted. Rather, modern people have largely become "global voyeurs," peering in through others' windows with fascination, but rarely gazing eye to eye in shared interest, connectedness, and understanding.[1]

The slow suffocation wrought by inattentiveness is terrible.

Mother Teresa, comparing the struggles of the poor in India to the very different sort of poverty common in rich nations, expressed, "As far as I'm concerned, the greatest suffering is to feel alone, unwanted, unloved. The greatest suffering is also having no one, forgetting what an intimate, truly human relationship is ..."

What we lack is captured in the words of novelist Taylor Caldwell: "The most desperate need of men today is not a new vaccine for any disease ... Man does not need to go to the moon or other solar systems. He does not require bigger and better bombs and missiles ... His real need, his most terrible need, is for someone to listen to him, not as a 'patient,' but as a human soul."[2] Have you noticed what happens when an attention-starved face is given the precious air it needs? Eyes spark. Hard faces soften. An irrepressible smile lightens over reddening lips, and a new eagerness buds like springtime.

Remarkably, even the least talented communicator, the

slow-tongued, the impossibly shy, can elicit such a response in others. To do so, we need offer one thing only: the pure oxygen of sincere attentiveness.

*   *   *   *

It was a Thursday afternoon, but the Sunday school classroom in the small urban church was full. Senator Tim Leslie's owlish eyes smiled out at the roomful of sharply-dressed African-Americans.

This was not familiar territory. Senator Leslie's home district was almost entirely white and rural. But several weeks before, as he pondered running for statewide office, his long-time friend Sam had delivered a challenge: "If you plan to represent the *whole* state as Lieutenant Governor, you'd better get to know the black community better." Tim accepted, and Sam arranged the gathering to introduce his friend to a number of his fellow pastors.

Receiving a nod from Sam, Tim began, "I appreciate you all coming to meet today. I've been looking forward to telling you a bit about my thoughts on what's right and what's wrong with our state, and what it needs ..."

An hour later, Tim was all smiles as he rounded the room, shaking hands with each pastor. He made it to the parking lot ahead of Sam and stood reviewing the experience. *Some great folks in there—and they seemed receptive to what I had to say.* He glanced hopefully at Sam as they slid into their seats. "Well?"

"You really want to hear?"

Tim's grin drooped, but he nodded. Sam shook his head. "I don't know, Tim. They appreciated you showing up, but ... well, there wasn't much beyond that. I'm sorry."

"Me too," muttered Tim, deflated. They traveled several miles in silence before Tim turned back to Sam. "Could we give it one more try?"

A month later, Tim sat at the head of another Sunday school room gathering. "I appreciate you coming to meet today," he began. "Sam helped set this up because I'd like to talk about our state and what it needs. So, we're going to go around the room, starting here on my left, sharing our thoughts on three questions ..."

Nearly everyone had spoken, some extensively, when Sam nudged Tim and pointed to his watch. It was past time for their next meeting. "I haven't spoken yet," whispered Tim. Sam shrugged apologetically. "We've got to go."

Sam thanked the group for gathering, and the two men began toward the door. Tim did not get three steps before finding himself surrounded. Pastor after pastor gripped him on the shoulders and pumped his hand. A woman in a broad red hat squeezed him in a bear hug. "This has been the best dialogue we've ever had!" she gushed. Voice after voice boomed the same thought.

> "The greatest gift that we can give one another is rapt attention to one another's existence."
>
> —Sue Atchley Ebaugh[3]

Tim was nearly dizzy by the time he made it to the car. Sam grinned. "Now *that* went well."

Tim shook his head, grinning as well. "I got an education in there. But was that a *dialogue*? I didn't even speak."

"You *heard* what they had to say. I could tell you were really listening. They could too. You listened with your heart. That's not something these folks have seen much of—especially from Legislator types like you."

Tim Leslie never became Lieutenant Governor. He lost the election by a narrow margin and returned to his post in the Legislature. But he says now that listening brought even better rewards. He gained lasting friendships, new perspective, and a deepened appreciation for a once-distant community.

Of course, it is not only urban pastors who desire to be heard, to be noticed, to be focused upon. From the glittering top of the social pyramid to its gritty basement, humans crave sincere attention. The results of a study of teenage prostitutes in San Francisco are recounted in the book *Am I Making Myself Clear?*[4] When asked what they lacked at home that caused them to run away, the girls' answers came down almost universally to three words: "Someone to listen."

At the other end of the social spectrum, the story is much the same. As a senior legislative staff member in California's Capitol recently confided, "Hardly anyone really listens around here. People act politely and nod at what you say, but they rarely really hear you. When someone does listen, it leaves a deep impression on me. I think to myself, 'Now *that* is a person I want to be around.'"

Even those who appear hopelessly hardened are often driven by the same need, sometimes even moreso than the rest of us. The words of former President Jimmy Carter from a 1994 interview with *Rolling Stone* are telling. Speaking of his experiences negotiating with the cruel dictators of small nations, he expressed, "Quite often ... these little guys, who might be

---

PERSONAL NOTES—Erik

Click. Click. Click. My agile thumbs type on my Blackberry keyboard, discretely placed just below the edge of the conference table. "Please send package to reporter." I hit send and lean back in my chair, returning my portable, attached-at-the-hip office to its holder. *Keeping the trains running,* I comfort myself, still not paying any attention to the person speaking at the end of the table. Buzz. Buzz. I feel two vibrations on my hip signaling a new message. Without hesitation, I scroll to the new email. This time it's from a friend. Again, without a second thought, I reply. "R u coming tonight?" There, another relationship maintained. Another colleague in the conference room speaks. My mind, however, is far from this room. I am needed, I remind myself, and I need to keep things moving. What is better —daydreaming or doing work? I hear my name. My head raises to see a room of eyes fixed upon me. "I'm sorry," I mutter, "Can you repeat that?" Someone else interjects the answer. I slowly slide the Blackberry back into its case and re-engage with the people in the room. The meeting is over. Buzz. Buzz. Another meeting to attend.

making atomic weapons or who might be guilty of some human rights violation ... are looking for someone to listen to their problems and help them communicate."[5]

The need is universal. Desperately so.

*   *   *   *

The throng poured through Jericho's gates, rolling out from the city in a tumult of noise and dust. At its ever-shifting center walked Jesus, the rabbi from Galilee. Even those watching from a distance could tell that each man, woman, and child wanted to press nearer to him, hear his replies, see what he would do next. Despite the crush of the crowd, he kept remarkable composure, interacting with those fortunate enough to thrust themselves within earshot.

People on the fringes scrambled along, hoping to catch just a glimpse or a phrase. A blind man seated on the roadside was not helping matters, shouting something in the unintelligible croak of an alms-seeker. "Quiet!" a large stonemason grunted. "I didn't leave the job site just to hear you barking."

The crowd brushed blind Bartimaeus by, offering only a mouthful of dust for his trouble. "Jesus, son of David," he called one last time.

"Don't waste your voice," someone shot back.

Suddenly, a hush rippled through the crowd. Jesus had stopped. He was saying something. What? Two young men began clearing a path out from the middle, back toward Bartimaeus. The beggar's blanched eyeballs turned skyward, his body trembling as he heard his name. "Bartimaeus, cheer up, Jesus is calling for you!" A half-dozen eager hands lifted him and tugged him forward, into the heart of the whispering crowd.

The hands fell away, and Bartimaeus stopped. Silence. Then a voice. "What do you want me to do for you?"

Bartimaeus' mind felt like it was tumbling down a hillside. *He's asking a question? To me? How did he hear me in the middle of all this?* His dusty mouth seemed to be full of wool. From the midst of the crowd, Jesus had somehow noticed him, a blind beggar, calling from the margins; now Jesus stood here next to him waiting, listening. *Does this great man really want me to answer, to hear from me?* The expectant silence made the answer clear.

It took a moment for Bartimaeus to realize that the next voice he heard was his own, "I ... I want to see ..."

*   *   *   *

Attentiveness may seem to be a passive quality. It is not. The sort Jesus practiced, at least, went far beyond the inert "receptivity" that absorbs only sounds and sights forceful enough to intrude upon the senses. It was *active*, watching and seeking, like the straining neck and twitching nostrils of a gazelle in lion country, like the sweeping eye of a searchlight.

This was more than a "skill." Jesus' attentiveness was a discipline, an intentional concentrating of the senses.

Most often, he turned this focus toward people or details others overlooked—the tossed-out, unlovely, disease-ridden, and rejected. He approached the seemingly irrelevant and expendable with a thoroughness that bestowed deep value and dignity. He emphasized the small and insignificant.

As much as any modern man, Jesus was immersed in the sort of dizzying activity that tends to numb us to life's subtle shades and drown out all but the loudest voices. Yet, somehow, in the grandness of his mission and purpose ... in all the demands upon his time ... in the seriousness of his words ... in the size of his following ... Jesus never overlooked the details of life.

In the midst of it all, he attuned his senses to the work of attentiveness. A diminutive tax collector up in a tree, a housewife drawing water from a well, lepers and social outcasts, mothers seeking blessings on their children—all caught Jesus' notice and received his unreserved attention.

Perhaps most remarkable of all, Jesus consistently revealed attentiveness in its highest form: empathy, an attentiveness of the heart.

Simply opening our eyes and ears to what is around us can be challenging enough. It is far more difficult to open our hearts to the deeper emotions and worries of others.

But such was Jesus' attentiveness. Time and again, the disciples noted Jesus' reaction to the rag-tag crowds and the hapless individuals who filled them. Writing about it years later, they consistently used the same word to describe it: "compassion"—not merely feeling sorry for, but feeling or even *suffering with*, a "co-passion."

At the tomb of Lazarus, Jesus displayed this quality with special poignancy. Although apparently having every intent of ending the cause of everyone's sadness, Jesus opened his heart to the ache of the moment and the anguish of those around him. There was no hint of distant, above-the-fray scrutiny. It was the full attentiveness of compassion, suffering with. And Jesus wept.

From first to last, attentiveness served as a wellspring of Jesus' communication. Always active. Always thorough. Listening and noticing, picking out and discerning, observing and questioning, seeking and even feeling.

*   *   *   *

A story is told of a woman who was taken to dinner by the great British Prime Minister William Gladstone. Not long after, the same lady dined with Gladstone's equally famous political nemesis, Benjamin Disraeli. Asked later about the impression the two prominent figures had made upon her, she explained, "When I left the dining room after sitting next to Mr. Gladstone, I thought he was the cleverest man in England. But after sitting next to Mr. Disraeli, I thought I was the cleverest woman in England."

What made the difference? We all know the answer. Attentiveness stirs us like nothing else in the world. It touches our deep longing for connectedness and intimacy, our ache to feel valued and to know that we are understood.

After the flashbulbs have exhausted themselves and the confetti is swept into a tidy pile, most people care little if you have built grand towers, scripted best sellers, or steered a Fortune 500 corporation. They want to know one thing: "Do you care about me?"

We are insecure, all of us, from the deaf janitor to the rock-jawed football coach. Frequently, the brighter a person's veneer of success and confidence, the more ravenous his hunger for affirmation. Pull back the orange peel just a bit, and you will find that each woman and man, no matter how polished or praised, is deep down a little girl longing to know that she is beautiful or worthy, or a little boy eager to hear that he is handsome or capable.

Of course, this need can be manipulated. Frequently it is. Feigned attentiveness can be an assassin's dagger in the hands of ambitious ladder-climbers, sexual predators, and other charlatans. Sincere attentiveness is another path altogether. It conveys genuine respect, concern, and value more than any other communication decision. When a person receives another's whole-hearted attention, suddenly they matter; they have worth. In a very real sense, at that moment, they feel they have been brought into existence.

That is why people respond to attentiveness almost as if to magic. It is a kiss that really does transform frogs into princes and princesses—changing behavior, opening hearts, and inspiring loyalty.

Attentiveness carries this potency wherever you go. Workers at the City Team Homeless Ministry in San Francisco, California, seek to meet the homeless' physical needs as best they can. But at the heart of their work, they report, is in striving to give their ragged, bleary-eyed patrons the personal notice they so rarely receive. Volunteers even wash the feet of the homeless, listening carefully to their stories, doing all they can to understand and even share the emotions of the human being before them. Admittedly, the homeless often offer little in return, but the sincere personal interest rarely fails to have an impact.

*   *   *   *

The benefits of attentiveness are not limited to those who receive the attention. The person giving it may gather even greater rewards. In the words of an old Turkish proverb, "To speak is to sow, to listen is to reap."

As communicators, attentiveness sharpens our effectiveness by giving us the lay of the land.

The best communication is never a "magic bullet"—a formula or string of words that, if properly launched, consistently delivers predictable results. The quest to express ideas or build rapport is much more like the wooing of a coy lover or an extended campaign to take a city. Such efforts demand continual responsiveness to the unique, evolving particulars of the situation and the people involved.

History's ash heap is littered with charismatic leaders who lacked attentiveness. There are monarchs like King Louis XIV of France or Russia's Tsar Alexander, who lost any connection with the experience of the people under their rule. There are generals, like Confederate George S. Pickett, who took little note of changing details on the field of battle and charged into ruin. There are generally decent managers who failed to observe low morale in their offices, and caring mothers who remained oblivious to the frustration caused by their smothering protectiveness.

Attentiveness is what enables us to discern which words and actions will best fit the uniqueness of each situation. Is this moonlit moment the right time to profess your love, or are breath mints necessary? Should you continue in your presentation, or perhaps give the audiences a stand-and-stretch break?

Attentiveness makes our communication living and responsive, capable of situation-specific creativity. If we are willing to act upon what we discover, attentiveness leads to well-wooed lovers and successful campaigns.

Attentiveness enriches our experience of the broader world as well.

Ralph Waldo Emerson wrote, "To the attentive eye, each moment of the year has its own beauty, and in the same field, it beholds, every hour, a picture which was never seen before, and which shall never be seen again."[6]

Whatever the situation, a posture of attentiveness makes experiences fuller and more meaningful. It stirs a childlike delight in the marvels of creation, from the amazing nano-technology in every living cell to the dizzying expanse of galaxies. It also offers insight into the nature of humankind—watching a love-struck couple in a coffee shop, or catching what is being said by a child's eyes.

To those who cultivate attentiveness, every interaction is an opportunity to learn. At the dull party, thoughtful questions turn the shy plumber into a trove of information about sinks and drains; at the less-than-inspiring company training day, one can still observe what it is that makes the better presentations better.

This nonstop inflow of knowledge, appreciation, and insight guarantees that the attentive person never grows stagnant. It continually washes away moldy assumptions and dried-out truisms, replacing them with the airy and original.

For the artist, this enriching flow is lifeblood.

The greatness of the masters—Van Gogh, Bach, Da Vinci, Tolstoy, Frost—came largely from their deep attentiveness. Life, people, and creation fascinated them, and their senses remained continually open and alert.

Don Postema, who served as chaplain at the University of Michigan for thirty-four years, expressed the thought well. To be truly great as creators and communicators, he observed, artists "need this kind of awareness to write, or paint, or draw with any authenticity. They need to *pay attention* ... They must take time to penetrate below the surface of things, to rediscover the world with an eye of love, and to 'see' into reality. Being an artist involves 'grasping life in its depth,' as the sensitive artist Vincent Van Gogh once wrote."[8]

> ## "Most people never listen."
>
> —Ernest Hemmingway[7]

An artist of communication—and each of us can be one—must do the same. Supplied in this way by the wellspring of attentiveness, our words never cease to reverberate with creativity, freshness, and life.

*   *   *   *

Even after we have committed ourselves to attentiveness, beauty, power, speed, and noise still tug viciously at our concentration. Urgency and the worries of life insist upon it. Amid even the most enjoyable conversations, self-interested thoughts still chatter on within our heads, sucking our attention selfishly inward: *How will this affect my plans? What will*

I do when this conversation is over ... next week ... for my vacation? It is almost inevitable that individuals who inhabit the margins, the quiet cries of human hearts, and all that is delicate, subtle, or less-than-stunning will end up unnoticed, calling feebly from the dusty roadside.

Merely desiring attentiveness will not be enough. We must *cultivate* it, as a young musician develops her ear for subtle notes and melodies. "To listen is an effort," stated composer Igor Stravinsky, "... just to hear is no merit. A duck hears also."[9]

But how? How do we truly listen and see in this way, as Jesus did, perceiving what others do not? The primary and most crucial aspect is deceptively simple: *We must first seek to be silent.*

Silence, explained philosopher Josef Pieper, "is the prerequisite of the apprehension of reality: only the silent hear and those who do not remain silent do not hear."[10] If we desire to listen to whispers, to discern those subtle things that do not simply barge in upon our senses, we must be willing to bite down with stern resolve upon our tongue.

PERSONAL NOTES—Jedd

Dinner was over, and the kitchen table was fast becoming a writer's junkyard of books, pens, and paper. Rachel, my wife, slid into the chair across from me to ask me a question.

I nodded in the affirmative, and she continued, conversing through an issue or two before inquiring, "So, what do you think?"

"I don't think I'd worry about it," I replied, looking up from the manuscript.

"Worry about what?"

"Worry about ... you know, what you said."

"And what was that?"

"Well," I stalled, trying to recall words I had heard but not processed. I had thought I was listening.

"You weren't listening," she stated flatly.

I began to protest, but she was right. Perhaps I could blunt the impact with a joke. "It's hard to listen when I'm working on a book about attentiveness," I offered with a grin. Rachel smiled, her eyes twinkling with the pleasure of having nabbed me, but I sensed a hint of disappointment as well.

This is the person I love most in the whole world. I delight to listen to Rachel as to no other; yet even with her, my attention can be inconsistent or distracted.

A former professor related to me how he traveled across the country recently, visiting old friends and acquaintances. They were all well-educated and polite people, who likely perceived themselves as good listeners. But after the pleasantries, it seemed that most wanted to talk about little but their own experiences and opinions. They hardly probed into his life at all.

Is it possible that all of us—even those who write or read about attentiveness—are often far less attentive than we imagine? In my case, I believe the answer is "yes."

This demands patience and self-control. Journalist Fran Lebowitz noted, "The opposite of talking isn't listening. The opposite of talking is waiting."[11] In an era that measures time in nanoseconds, waiting can be painful. But as we do quietly wait, our senses begin to open and notice. Meanwhile, the invitation presented by our attentive silence draws others to open themselves to us.

The most potent kind of silence, however, requires more than just not talking. We must have an inner disposition of stillness as well. When our mind is overwhelmed with activity or buzzing with internal noise—even if we are outwardly silent—we tend to notice only things that promise immediate satisfaction of our own self-focused interests. In contrast, inward silence allows a sensitivity to the subtle. We begin to hear not only words, but also what is being said between them.

This inner quietness, as we will explore further in Chapter 6, is formed especially in solitude, reflection, and prayer. In such times, we begin to still the inner noise that makes full attentiveness almost impossible. This second silence comes slowly, and with effort. Annie Dillard described her own struggle to "gag the commentator, to hush the noise of useless babble that keeps me from seeing just as surely as a newspaper dangled before my eyes. The effort is really a discipline requiring a lifetime of dedicated struggle."[12]

The reward, however, is worth the labor.

Silence, properly cultivated, prepares us for an attentiveness that goes beyond merely noticing details. It starts us on a path of perceptivity to the deeper, often-hidden realities of our friends, children, audiences, and even life itself. The result, as Don Postema observed, is often "a deep insight into reality, a capacity to see beneath the surface of nature and people, an awareness that uncovers for us a spiritual vitality in our world, in ourselves—and points us toward God."[13]

*   *   *   *

Given how much most people long to express themselves, silence is often all that is needed to draw a person out and build meaningful connection. As already noted, though, Jesus didn't stop here. His attentiveness was not passive, like an unmoving satellite dish that absorbs only the signals strong enough to drown out the others. His attention was deliberate, vigorous, and discerning.

A number of disciplines can help us grow in this character trait, building from silence into the active attentiveness Jesus modeled.

1. *Make question-asking an art.* Jesus often anchored his communication in thoughtful questions. Prior to interactions, think through questions you can ask to dig beneath trite exchanges and into meaningful discussion. Try viewing yourself like a reporter, seeking to draw out significant thoughts and experiences from others.

2. *Sacrifice distractions.* As much as we imagine no one notices, multi-tasking *always* diminishes attentiveness. Shut off cell phones and the background TV, place the newspaper on the ground, and turn away from the computer while on the phone. Removing distractions enhances our perceptivity. Equally important, by making these "sacrifices," we show we're serious about listening.

3. *Involve the whole body.* Physical stance can have a surprising impact on interactions. Consider how kneeling for prayer, although not necessary, can orient us toward humility and receptiveness. In much the same way, posture can prepare us for attentiveness: Force your eyes not to rove; set shoulders square toward the other; avoid crossing your arms. These physical actions express interest and help us remain focused and engaged.

4. *Confirm your perceptions.* Even the most discerning observer can misconstrue what she hears or sees. Simple inquiries—"You look frustrated. Are you down?"—can help clarify our perceptions. Communication experts call this practice "active listening." Asking for confirmation ("Do you mean ...?") or repeating back a form of what you think you heard ("So you're telling me ...?") ensures we understand what is being said and also conveys to others that we care about they are saying.

5. *Cultivate attentiveness by taking special note of people on the margins.* Jesus directed his attentiveness especially toward the "invisible" men and women of his day: the poor, ostracized, and chronically ill. Try giving special attention to people others overlook—yard workers, janitors, the disabled, or homeless. Beyond merely developing our own attentiveness, this choice will give affirmation and "oxygen" to people who need it greatly.

6. *Learn to see.* This does not just mean "learn how to see better," but rather, *"gain knowledge that will enable you to see more."* A boy who has no knowledge of forests will likely "see" nothing on a mountainside except "a bunch of trees." With a little study, though, suddenly every pine, cedar, and dogwood grows distinct. Now, he *can't help* but see them. The same is true as we learn the family, culture, or life story of an individual. Whether gained through books, classes, or conversations, new learning increases our ability to see.

7. *Express what you observe.* Annie Dillard writes, "Seeing is of course very much a matter of verbalization. Unless I call my attention to what passes before my eyes, I simply won't see it." The practice of articulating things we've noticed—thanking a waitress' manager for her effort, mentioning a talent you per-

ceive in a friend, or remarking on the smile of a supermarket clerk—makes this things more real for us, and also gives gifts to others.

If practiced, these disciplines enable us to give ourselves wholly to each situation and person we encounter.

Initially, a sense of *effort* will be continual. Like pulling back on the chain of an overeager puppy, we must repeatedly draw our attention back into the moment, dragging our focus away from *everything else* that tugs at our thoughts—and on to the person immediately before us.

Over time, however, disciplines become habits, and habits become character. Attentiveness will no longer be a straining decision, but second nature. Perhaps for the first time, we can begin to dwell in the present.

"I believe in being fully present," Morrie said in *Tuesdays with Morrie*.[14] Life and relationships had grown clearer to the dying professor, and he explained to his younger friend gently, "That means you should be with the person you're with. When I am talking to you now, Mitch, I try to keep focused only on what is going on between us. I am not thinking about something we said last week. I am not thinking of what's coming up this Friday ... I am talking to you. I am thinking about you."

As difficult as it is to root ourselves in the present, it is the only place we can attend to others ... or, for that matter, really live at all. In the words of missionary martyr Jim Elliot, "Wherever you are, be all there."[15]

*   *   *   *

There was no question that the matter was urgent. The daughter of an influential man lay on death's door. With the desperation only a father could know, he had begged Jesus to come—*quickly*. A large crowd pressed close as the two men set off together at a rapid clip. No one wanted to miss what would happen next.

They had traveled some distance when Jesus came to a sudden stop, bringing the whole procession to an off-balance halt.

"Who touched me?" he asked, gazing into the crowd. Eyebrows rose, and onlookers chuckled. Amid this throng, *anyone* could have touched him. But Jesus searched on, face after face, seeking a telltale gesture or trace of emotion.

From out of the crowd, a woman tumbled to the ground in front of him. Her tear-streaked face appeared weary, as old sandstone. "It was me," she choked, "I grasped your robe— only for a moment."

The riddle was solved. People shrugged and began moving forward, anxious to get to the more pressing matter ahead. What more could she want? As witnesses later reported, just touching the edge of Jesus' robe had apparently produced the healing the woman believed she'd come for. But Jesus knew better. He held up his hand, stilling the crowd and inviting the woman to speak.

Hesitant, she searched his face. Sensing the invitation was sincere, she began, pouring out her life's story in detail for perhaps the first time: twelve long years of chronic bleeding, swindlers whose costly treatments only increased the pain, medical bills sucking away the last of her resources, the burning loneliness of social rejection ...

Her words flowed freely until there were no more. She gazed at Jesus, her eyes moist and unburdened. Jesus smiled. "Daughter, your faith has healed you. Go in peace." Only now would he return to the urgent matter at hand.

Attentiveness, more often than not, is most needed when it is least convenient.

Facing interruption and intrusion, we discover where our commitments lie. The costs can be high. As a busy lawyer expressed, "I frequently find my *in*attentiveness due in large part to wanting to stay on schedule. Or I'm on the clock and want to keep my time productive. So I avoid or cut off personal conversations with clients and staff. Attentiveness requires sacrificing your goals, agenda, schedule, deadlines, and efficiency. It might mean your whole afternoon gets thrown off when you encounter someone starved for attention."

Of course, even an attentive person must sometimes draw boundaries or bring a rambling conversation to an end. Jesus' choices, however, show that he placed an almost disturbing premium on attentiveness. He apparently believed it was worth a delay in his mission to a dying child—simply to provide the oxygen of attentiveness to a woman others had discarded.

Following Jesus' pattern in this is subversive. To place such value on attention-giving is an act of treason against values and habits that stand as pillars of our culture. Attentiveness upends the sacrosanct priority normally given to efficiency, accomplishment, self-expression, and seeing days go just-as-planned.

If we choose this path, some of the things we would prefer to hold tightly may indeed be lost. The person before us, however, will receive what they so desperately need: our full attention—ears and eyes, heart and soul.

*　　　*　　　*　　　*

As a final note, a word of warning. Attentiveness is a potent commodity. It is pure oxygen in a room choked with carbon dioxide, fresh air to the suffocating. As such, attentiveness can dramatically increase our capacity for influence. Realizing this, we may be tempted to use attentiveness falsely, to exert it as a tool for our own self-absorbed ends.

But true attentiveness cannot be faked. We can, of course, learn techniques that make us appear attentive: managing our facial expressions, keeping eye contact, mirroring the other person's body language. These practices are not wrong in themselves, but if they spring from nothing more than selfishness or ambition, people will eventually notice. When they do, all we hoped to accomplish through our carefully packaged "attentiveness" will unravel like a cheap stuffed animal won at the carnival.

Real attentiveness can have but one source: a sincere concern for those with whom we communicate.

If anything else is motivating us, we will likely abandon attentiveness just when it is most needed. Only a genuine care for others enables us to value hearing more than being heard, to extend our focus beyond our own petty concerns, to prize the opportunity to know a person's heart and open ourselves to experiencing what they feel.

Mere technique will never take us this far. Attentiveness must flow sincerely from the heart. When it does, new life always follows.

TAKE IT WITH YOU …

Know that what will determine the success of your communication, far more than whether others notice and hear you, is whether you truly notice and hear others.

Silence is the first step, "the prerequisite of the apprehension of reality." As an exercise, try to go through a conversation speaking only when necessary, not bringing up any of your own ideas.

Build on silence by training yourself for active attentiveness. This effort will bring immediate results, but is honed over a lifetime. Choose one or two of the seven disciplines mentioned in the chapter to engage this week.

Most of us imagine ourselves to be good listeners. Question yourself. Do others come out of interactions with you feeling that you really sought to hear them and draw them out?

Remember: You have a desperately needed gift to offer through attentiveness. Many are gasping for it. Even to the confident and secure, it will be a prized blessing.

In a Media Age,
we assume that ...
Effective communication must come
from a position of power.

In Every Age,
the truth is ...
The best communication
requires drawing near,
whatever the cost.

CHAPTER TWO

SEEKING CONNECTION:
On Their Turf and in Their Terms

Professor Leo Buscaglia recounts the true story of a little boy whose neighbor's wife passed away. Seeing that the elderly man was heartbroken and grieving, the boy's mother warned her son not to bother the neighbor.

It wasn't long before the mother noticed the little boy crossing into the neighbor's yard and climbing up into the old man's lap. He remained there for some time, sitting quietly.

When the boy returned home, his mother met him with her hands on her hips. "I told you not to bother him!" she scolded. "What were you doing?"

"I wasn't doing anything," the little fellow answered. "I was just helping him cry."

Communication does not begin with words; it begins with connection.

Commands and demands delivered from a position of power may drive the course of lives and events for a time. But they are feeble in their influence over hearts and minds, and their impact fades with the passing of those who spoke them.

True communication is another matter. It is, first and foremost, about *connecting*, coming together, the sharing of life and self, a seeking to know and be known.

Whether on the mass scale or the most personal, communication is born as two human souls come close and touch. To begin, the communicator must enter the space and language of another.

*   *   *   *

Molokai. The island's name was pronounced bitterly, with loathing and fear. Between 1866 and 1873, nearly eight hundred lepers were quarantined there on an isolated peninsula. Towering volcanic cliffs hemmed them in on three sides, and crashing surf on the fourth. It was a prison, a netherworld made all the more surreal by its pacific beauty.

Abandoned without law or hope, the lepers gave themselves alternately to despair and to what pleasures they could grasp. Robbery and drunkenness, sexual orgies and anarchy marked their lives. When finally, after a tortuous descent, the lepers finally succumbed to their disease, their already-decayed bodies often became food for pigs and wild dogs.

Father Damien first came to Hawaii in 1864. He had been born in Europe, the sturdily built son of a well-to-do Belgian farmer. When his brother fell ill and could not travel to his post at Hawaii's Sacred Heart Mission, Damien asked to take his place.

For a decade, Damien served at the mission. During that time, many of his parishioners were forced away to Molokai. Their memory remained wedged in his mind, slowly building into a fearsome emotion. He yearned to go to the lepers and to convey love to them where they lived. In April of 1873, Father Damien wrote to his superiors, asking for permission.

A month later, he stood on the beaches of the dreaded isle.

Damien steeled himself for the worst, but the sights and smells of Molokai left him gasping. One of his first encounters was with a young girl, her body already half eaten by worms. One by one, Damien set out to meet them all. Carefully avoiding physical contact, he confronted their rotting bodies, putrid breath, and the ever-present rasped coughing.

Damien's first desire was to remind the lepers of their inherent dignity as children of God. To demonstrate the value of their lives, he honored their deaths—constructing coffins, digging graves, protecting the cemetery from scavenging animals, and ensuring a ceremony for every passing.

As the days went by, however, Damien began to feel that he could not fully convey all that he wished to share without drawing ever nearer. He began timidly to touch the lepers. He ate with them, and hugged them. Over time, he even began to clean and wrap their oozing sores. Everything Damien did, he did with the lepers. Together, they built coffins and chapels, cottages and roads. He taught them how to farm, raise animals, and even sing despite their mangled vocal chords. One report described him teaching two lepers to play the organ with the ten fingers they still had between them.

Damien sought to draw near to the lepers in his words as well, even speaking of "*we* lepers." Writing to his brother in Europe, he explained, "I make myself a leper with the lepers to gain all to Jesus Christ. That is why, in preaching, I say 'we lepers'; not 'my brethren ...'"

It was eleven years after Damien's arrival on Molokai that he spilled boiling water on his leg. He watched with horror as his feet blistered—yet felt no pain. His efforts to draw ever nearer to the lepers was complete. Now he would meet them in their disease as well.

The final five years of his life, Damien served the lepers of

Molokai as a leper priest. The days passed with both joy and suffering. Outpourings of international support arrived at the island, and also several helpers. Alongside the blessings, however, came physical pain, and times of loneliness and even depression. Finally, on April 15, 1889, Damien breathed his last. He was laid to rest among the thousands of lepers he had helped to bury in what he called his "garden of the dead."

> **"In the Christian story God descends to reascend. He comes down ... to the very roots and sea-bed of the Nature he has created ..."**
>
> —C.S. Lewis, in *Miracles*[1]

In 1936, at the request of the Belgian government, Father Damien's body was returned to his birthplace. Years later, the people of Molokai pleaded that at least part of their beloved Father be returned to them. What they finally received, with joy, was Damien's right hand—the hand that had touched and soothed and embraced them, even when everyone else had done all they could to keep the lepers far away.

*   *   *   *

Communication. Community. Compassion. Communion. Obviously, these words grow with their roots entwined. All of them spring from the Latin term, *com*, together. The word "communication" is itself from the Latin *communicare*, meaning "to share together," or, more literally, "to make common."

To our loss, we often define it otherwise. Many textbooks focus on communication as little more than the transmission and reception of information. With such an emphasis, little matters except the bytes and bits we are working to insert into others' brains and the reaction we hope to create. The issue of connectedness fades to the background, valued only as a tool to be exploited. Viewed in this way, communication becomes an impersonal exchange of messages, a one-way street where, as author Margaret Miller described, "conversations are simply monologues delivered in the presence of a witness."[2]

True communication, however, is never monologue; it is dialogue, the *coming together* of two living beings, even when separated by chasms of culture and language, age and distance, opinion and race.

This connection, just as with electric lines, is the fundamental necessity of communication. Without connection, exchange is impossible, no matter how high the voltage. But when the wires touch, energy crackles, and life begins to *flow*.

Great communicators, before anything else, seek means of connection.

Father Damien did just that. He came near to the lepers, in every way he knew how. He dwelt in their space, spoke their language, addressed their most pressing needs, and even tasted their pain. To the fullest extent possible, he entered their turf and dealt in their terms. And as these connection points between Damien and the lepers sparked, the truths and affection he wished to convey flowed between them, like electricity.

This work of coming near for the sake of connection is the foundation of all fruitful communication.

It is also inescapably at the heart of Christian faith. As Jesus' closest friend, the Apostle John, described of Jesus' life, "The Word became flesh and dwelt among us …"[3] That which was far off, removed, and distinct came near. He dwelt in our space, spoke human language, addressed our most pressing needs, and even tasted our pain.

From his first screamed breaths in dank barnyard air, to his last pain-wracked gasps on the cross, Jesus' life was continually a work of connecting to those he sought to reach. His every act of communication, whether verbal or otherwise, was anchored in choices to connect with his audience—always moving *toward*, reaching *into*, drawing *from* their daily experiences.

*   *   *   *

Julius charged through the crowded streets of Capernaum, his sword clattering at his side. Townspeople averted their eyes as the Roman officer approached, but stared with wonder as his long legs carried him away. It was not every day that a soldier of his rank traveled with such undignified haste.

Merchants and customers parted as Julius plowed into the teeming marketplace. A beak-nosed shopkeeper jumped as he felt a hand fall on his shoulder. He glanced up, cringing slightly, but saw only earnest question in the soldier's eyes. "Have you seen him?" Julius gasped. Tongue-tied, the shopkeeper shook his head.

A small girl, more perceptive, or perhaps braver than the other onlookers, pointed up the street. "He's coming this way," she piped. Julius tendered a smile in thanks, then burst off in the direction the child had indicated.

A short distance away, he spotted a throng, flowing toward him through the overcrowded street like a flooding river. To his surprise, the people did not melt away before him. With everyone so intent on the man at the center, Julius became just another onlooker, quickly entangled within the mass.

Wedging himself between bodies and pulling on shoulders, Julius moved inward. On tiptoes he could catch glimpses of the unremarkable figure in the middle of it all. "*Could this be him?*" he mused. "*Jesus of Nazareth?*"

As he neared the center, some of the crowd members finally

noticed who he was. A corridor formed between the smooth-faced soldier and the bearded man in the middle. Several disciples stepped forward, filling the gap and broadening their chests, ready for a confrontation.

"Lord ..." Julius said, breathing hard. The crowd stilled. "My servant lies at home paralyzed and in terrible suffering."

Jesus' eyes remained on the soldier. Without hesitating, he replied, "I will go and heal him." A buzz of approval rippled through the crowd—they wanted to see another miracle.

But Julius shook his head, gently touching Jesus' shoulder. "Lord, I do not deserve to have you come under my roof. But just say the word, and my servant will be healed."

The disciples turned to one another, whispering guesses of what Jesus would do.

Jesus nodded, a smile breaking onto his face. Nowhere in all of his travels had he encountered faith like this. "Go," he said. "It will be done just as you believed it would ..."

This story is often recounted as a testament to the remarkable faith of a Roman soldier. And that it is. But it also casts a spotlight on Jesus' readiness and desire to enter into the space of others. At a moment's notice, he was willing to venture out to the home of a complete stranger. The narrative highlights the significance of a man of his standing visiting a Roman manor, let alone entering the crude home of a laborer or the residence of a moral outcast. Even a Roman officer, a leader among Galilee's occupying overlords, felt he was unworthy to have Jesus enter his home.

Yet this was Jesus' way, the very core of his communication.

Through every means at his disposal, Jesus drew near to those with whom he sought to communicate. Simple, descriptive phrases from the Gospels capture this approach, startling only for their ordinariness:

Jesus went throughout Galilee, teaching in their synagogues ...

Jesus reached out his hand and touched the leper ...

While Jesus was having dinner at Matthew's house, many tax collectors and sinners came and ate with him ...

When Jesus entered the ruler's house ...

Jesus went through all the towns and villages ...

When Jesus came into Peter's house, he saw Peter's mother-in-law lying in bed with a fever. He touched her hand ...

He went in and reclined at the table ...

Coming to his hometown, he began teaching the people in their synagogue ...

He dined with the wealthy as a guest at their feasts. He conversed with religious leaders in their synagogues and temples. The poor he sought out in their alleys and gutters, the destitute on their sickbeds. Even the outcasts and the immoral encountered Jesus at their sides, in their homes, at their tables.

"They stoop to rise ..."

—Henry David Thoreau, in "Autumnal Tints"[4]

The residue of Palestine's dusty roads coated Jesus' feet. He breathed the sour odors of the crowds. Fishing boats and hillsides served as his platform as often as pulpits or podiums. The unlovely received his gaze; the untouchable felt his hands.

Even his words were distinctly *near* to his audiences. He spoke not with ivory tower phrases and abstract doctrines. Instead, he painted vivid word pictures that could be touched and tasted and smelled: baking yeast, a field of wheat, sheep and goats, falling towers, zesty salt, and scintillating light. And, always, he returned to stories—a form as accessible to children and the illiterate as to the educated elite.

No matter what audience, Jesus continually conveyed *his* message in *their* terms on *their* turf.

Can we do it like him? Absolutely. But be warned—it will require risk and even loss. Modern communication operates under the assumption that our words will be most potent when delivered from a position of power. Even when we recognize that connection is necessary, we seek it without releasing our grip on status, reputation, and comfort. No need to get too close, we believe. No need to lower ourselves. We seek impact without involvement, like a busy executive sending an assistant to pick up their sick child from school.

Real connection is never so safe or cost-free.

*   *   *   *

"I may be compelled to face danger, but never fear it, and while our soldiers can stand and fight, I can stand and feed and nurse them," vowed Clara Barton, the "angel in the battlefield" who joined fallen Civil War soldiers at the front lines to tend their wounds and whisper words of peace.[5]

Adorned in her trademark bonnet, red bow, and dark skirt, Clara arrived at the northern edge of Antietam's infamous "Cornfield" just after noon. Only days before, the field had been lush with towering stalks; now bodies crisscrossed the land amid the matted corn.

Nearby, harried surgeons wrapped soldiers' wounds with cornhusks. The army's medical supply wagons had been left far behind by the rapid march of the soldiers. Urged on by Clara, however, her own wagon had driven all night to get closer to the front of the line. Surgeons voiced their gratitude as she handed them the bandages and other medical supplies she had personally gathered over the past year.

Soon, Clara herself was wading out into the field. Between the whistle of bullets and thunder of cannons, feeble voices called out for death. Kneeling over a disoriented soldier, she cut back his wool pants to reveal an oozing wound. She lifted his head with her hand and offered him drink from a canteen, the only pain reliever she could offer as she prepared to operate.

Feeling something brush by her arm, Clara glanced down. A bullet had ripped through her sleeve. The weight of the man's head increased in her hand, and she realized the slug had pierced him, ending his life.

The hours passed quickly as Clara and her assistants moved from one man to the next. Again and again she stood, wiping caked blood and mud from her hands against her skirt, calling out for a stretcher.

As night fell, the fading light began to slow the work of the surgeons. From her wagon, Clara produced lanterns. As soldiers returned to their campfires, she remained with the wounded, working through the night.

Within a few days after the battle, medical supplies were in plenty. Exhausted, Barton collapsed from lack of sleep and an emerging case of typhoid fever. She was laid in the back of a wagon for the journey back to Washington. It was not long, however, before she regained her strength and returned to the battlefields of the Civil War.

Clara Barton later became the first president of the Red Cross. Throughout her life, her focus remained with the people suffering at the frontlines of wars and disasters. Coming into the troubled space of the desperate with aid and mercy was the hallmark of her life.

Before anything else, connection requires *drawing near*, through whatever means available.

This was Jesus' way. "The Word became flesh and *dwelt among* us." The term "dwelt" literally means, "to pitch a tent." Jesus was not a commuter, coasting in from distant suburbs to a downtown jobsite or a once-a-week ministry in the inner city. Like Barton, he set up camp, pitched his tent, right smack dab in the middle of the people he desired to reach.

Whatever the cost, this quest to *draw near* marks all who effectively connect.

The effort to draw near marked not only Jesus' actions and mental focus; it defined his words as well. Virtually every page of the Gospels bears a parable Jesus told. In fact, as described by the tax collector-turned-disciple Matthew, Jesus hardly said anything at all without using a parable. We tend to think of parables as stories with a moral theme. Indeed, most of Jesus' parables were stories. However, the description Matthew applied carries a fuller meaning. What formed the foundation of Jesus' communication was literally *para* (near) *ballo* (to bring)—"near-bringers."

A *paraballo* is any story or phrase that connects a distant, hard-to-visualize thought or concept with something vivid and familiar. Jesus never forced his listeners to wade off into the realm of abstract principles and doctrines. Instead, he brought the ideas he wished to convey close to them. Using these "near-bringers," he imbedded lofty ideas and principles into the dust and grime of the people's workaday lives.

The need for this sort of *near bringing* communication may seem obvious, but as teachers, managers and parents, we consistently fail in this regard.

Sometimes, this may be intentional—burnishing our image with large words and complex language. More often, though, we simply do not think about it. By default, we express ourselves in words and phrases familiar to us, without pondering whether or not they connect with others in meaningful ways.

Scientists find it hard to avoid technical jargon. Ph.D.s traffic in arcane phrases and gobbledygook. Pastors wrap simple truths in Byzantine doctrines, while their parishioners trade clichés that sound hollow and trite to the uninitiated. Jesus' approach was just the opposite. He continually sought to bring his communication closer, to make it accessible to any listener who sincerely desired to hear what he had to say. Four qualities in particular accomplished this:

Narrative. Love for stories is universal. Says writer A.S. Byatt, "Narration is as much a part of human nature as breath and the circulation of the blood."[6] Jesus harnessed stories as his primary means of communication, telling tales of kindly Samaritans and forgiving fathers, buried treasure and mouth-watering feasts. Whether Galilean farmers or jaded American teens, *everyone* delights in a tale well told.

Simplicity. Jesus' themes were grand and expansive. But he always offered truth in bite-sized chunks even illiterate laborers could digest. His language was never bookish or thick with theological jargon. Granted, sometimes even Jesus' disciples were so wrapped up in worn-out assumptions that they missed his points. Many still do today.[7]

Even so, multitudes of poor laborers, lowly peasants, and children gathered to listen to Jesus for days on end. Those

---

PERSONAL NOTES—Jedd

My dad's parents were out for the evening when he took the family station wagon for an illicit drive. He was thirteen.

The next day, the headline in the small town newspaper read, "Joy Ride Ends in Cold Bath." The station wagon had taken a curve too fast and rolled several times before landing in a creek. My dad was fortunate to escape with only bruises and scratches.

My grandfather, Dr. Medefind, likely could have protected my dad from legal penalties for the wreck, but he didn't. He believed consequences should be faced, even if that meant time in Juvenile Hall.

When my dad appeared before the judge, though, he was not alone. As he took his place in front of the bench, my grandfather stood up beside him.

"What do you plead?" came the voice from above.

It was not my dad, but my grandfather who replied. "Your Honor, we did wrong ..."

My grandfather passed away several years ago, but my father says that simple statement still echoes for him. With a simple choice of words, the father staked his tent beside the son, even in his guilt. It is the kind of drawing near that a thirteen-year-old boy never forgets.

who sincerely desired to learn never left empty handed.

Familiarity. Jesus' communication was consistently fashioned from the stuff of his listeners' everyday lives. He drew from their history, their Scriptures, their daily experiences, and from current events with which almost every listener would certainly have been familiar. People feel comfortable and connected when they hear references to things they recognize and interact with regularly.

Concreteness. Even when speaking of the lofty and eternal, Jesus never allowed his ideas to become disconnected from the realm of the concrete. He translated each concept into vivid images: a man plucking out his eyes, moths and rust devouring horded wealth, pigs trampling pearls. When possible, he involved physical examples as well—a small child, a coin, a man with a withered hand. Jesus made everything he spoke about real and tangible.

Communication that is simple, familiar, concrete, and makes ample use of stories—whether addressed to a large stadium or the junior higher next door—brings us near to our listeners. It connects us to them and their world.

*   *   *   *

Drawing near is the first point of connection. Proximity alone, however, is rarely enough. Having come close by, we must still work to build full connectedness.

As John described, Jesus not only drew near, he also became flesh.

Becoming flesh. Putting on skin. Wrapping elusive truth with cartilage and muscle, tendons and veins. This is the Christian faith's grandest enigma and wonder. Shockingly, an infinite God chose to speak not with lightening-bolt edicts or thundered commands. Instead, He enmeshed the transcendent *Word* within a human body, making what was distant and abstract now scandalously tangible.

The goal was clear. No medium could possibly be more accessible and familiar to humans than humanness.

To communicate, God wrapped all that He desired to convey into physical, touchable flesh.

Such an act is a great mystery indeed. Yet this putting of flesh upon the far-off and hard-to-grasp is required of all communicators. Without it, our words remain no more capable of touching others than disembodied specters.

So how do we do this? How does our communication become an act of enfleshment? How do we *incarnate* the things we wish to express in a way that can be touched and handled by our friends or spouse, students or employees?

Both the communicator and the communication must *take on flesh*.

*   *   *   *

INCARNATION THROUGH SHARED EXPERIENCE

Nothing allows a communicator to "take on flesh" like shared experience. Soldiers who have fought together, an athletic team at the end of a season, or a collection of strangers who have endured a long, hard bus ride together feel an almost mystical connection. Even individuals who have had similar experiences in the past—having faced poverty, grown up overseas, or fought cancer—share special bonds.

These connections allow for rich communication. This is because most of us assume, usually correctly, that those who have "walked a mile in our shoes" will understand us and care about the same things we do. So we tend to listen more readily and add weight to their words.

McDonald's Corporation requires individuals who wish to become franchise owners to spend time working the front lines of a restaurant's operations. Not only does this practice give would-be investors a better sense of how to manage their future business, but it also provides a basis for understanding and connecting to the people who will work for them.

Whenever possible, good communicators do the same—choosing to engage in activities that will give them a point of connection and shared experience.

INCARNATION THROUGH CULTURE AND CUSTOM

Sharing experiences is the fullest form of incarnation, but it is not always possible or realistic. A wealthy New Yorker will likely never fully know the taste of urban poverty, or what it was like to grow up in rural Iowa. Yet despite this, communicators can still take on others' flesh by adopting some of their customs or symbols. By honoring the things others value, we convey

---

PERSONAL NOTES—Erik

Long, hot summer days reddened the skin and blistered the hands. It was hard work on the construction site, but these friendly day-laborers, mostly Hispanic, never complained. They would laugh and tell stories, wipe their sweaty brow with dirt-caked hands, and more than earn their pay by day's end.

My father, the senior project manager, often chose to work "in the field" rather than in the air-conditioned offices of the corporate headquarters. He preferred a tool belt to a cell phone, and a T-shirt to the collared dress shirt his bosses required. He was quick to help the day-laborers carry lumber or dig ditches, telling them jokes in his broken Spanish. It was not for show; no one back at the office would know about this. It was, he says, because the hands-on work reminded him of the back-breaking labor he used to do, and also that there was as much value in digging a foundation as in meeting with city officials.

My father-in-law is the same way. A corporate executive in Los Angeles, he never forgot his modest beginnings. He was well-liked by everyone—from vice-presidents to janitorial staff—because he treated everyone the same. In fact, none of his fellow execs knew that he liked to share a six-pack of beers with the maintenance staff in the concrete bowels of the building, where the smell of sweat and cleaning supplies filled the air. It wasn't an attempt to "build teamwork" or give slaps on the back. He did it because he loved people—no matter what they did or where they worked in the building.

that we desire to connect with them and respect them as individuals.

Hudson Taylor remade Christian missions through his decisions to incarnate himself in this way. Most missionaries to China in the mid-1800's retained Western ways, wore English suits, and lived in homes like those back in England or America. After beginning much the same way, Taylor realized he would connect with the Chinese far more if he took on their culture. He became fluent in Mandarin and a second local dialect, adopted the robe and satin shoes worn by Chinese teachers, and grew his hair into the standard queue. He even allowed his fingernails to grow long, as other Chinese teachers did to show that they were scholars. It is said that literally millions of Chinese today trace their Christian faith back to this slight, humble man. Rather than communicating from the position of power and superior status considered birthright to British citizens, Taylor followed Jesus' pattern, incarnating himself into Chinese culture.

Of course, if we adopt symbols or customs merely as a tool of influence, with little sincerity or concern for the people involved, it may well backfire. Some say Michael Dukakis cost himself the 1988 presidential election when he tried to appear pro-military by riding in a tank dressed in soldier's gear. Images of Dukakis bouncing around with his helmet hanging down over his eyes suggested to both the military and the American people little but opportunism. Incarnation is anything but pretending to be something you are not.

Sincere efforts, though, even if awkward, will ultimately bear fruit. A young American who plans to move to the Middle East has chosen to give up pork and alcohol, grow a beard, study Mid-Eastern history, and takes other steps to honor the traditions of the Islamic world. Even in

California, his simple choices have produced connection with Muslim acquaintances and opened opportunities for deeper friendship.

INCARNATION THROUGH SELF-DISCLOSURE

Despite the unavoidable differences between any two people, our deeper parts are knit of the same material. Most of us readily find pieces of our own story in the tales of Helen of Troy, Lancelot, King David, or Abigail Adams. Is it not certain, then, that we can discover at least as many points of commonality with the people living around us today? As Frederick Buechner wrote, "… [T]he story of any one of us is in some measure the story of us all."[8]

Seeking out and revealing this commonality is a work of incarnation. It is often as simple as sharing honestly from our own lives and stories, especially when we speak with transparency about our hopes and failures, rough edges and desires. As we offer glimpses of the fact that we, too, experience these realities, we take on flesh in our audience's eyes. As some would say, we are showing our human side. This revealing of humanness brings us nearer, creating commonality and connection.

A brief anecdote is often all that is needed to connect in this way. The account need not be a war story, even if speaking with a veteran. It is enough to describe what it felt like when you failed your first high school exam, or how you lay beside your German Shepherd when it was hit by a car. A simple, personal story or a moment of vulnerable honesty can quickly turn you from a shadowy and distant figure into a flesh-and-blood companion with shared hopes and struggles.

*   *   *   *

The film, *The Mission*, opens as a Jesuit priest is being bound to a crude cross by South American Indians and thrown into a river. The man bumps and spins helplessly through turgid, chocolate waters, finally plunging to his death over roaring falls.

Learning of what has occurred, the priest's superior, Father Gabriel, pledges to venture up into the dense jungle above the falls. He will seek out this tribe, the Guarani, and attempt to reach out to them with the grace of Christ.

An arduous journey brings Gabriel and two companions to the foot of the falls, where they build a monument to their slain brother. Then Gabriel proceeds alone, scraping his way upward beside the crushing flow of water.

Cresting the top of the falls, Gabriel knows the danger has only begun. It is Guarani territory, and the mottled green around him will soon glint with dark eyes and arrow points. Gabriel does not speak a word of the tribe's dialect, so he must find some other means of connection. Failure guarantees death.

He sits on a large stone and removes the cloth from a slender parcel he's had slung over his shoulder, an oboe. Fingers trembling, Gabriel brings it to his lips. One note, then another. A haunting tune rises into the jungle canopy and filters out over tangled trails.

The eyes and gleaming blades Gabriel has expected soon appear in the shadows. A moment later, the squat, dark-skinned men emerge, their black hair painted with stripes of maroon—the Guarani. It is clear they find the sound pleasing, mesmerizing. As Gabriel well knows, the Indians of the region delight in music.

One stocky Guarani steps forward, his face twisted in a scowl. He grabs the oboe as if it were a viper, then breaks it over his knee. Fear tightens Gabriel's face. A moment later, however, another native picks the broken instrument from the ground. He places its broken ends together and hands it to the priest, motioning for him to play. Gabriel blows into the end, but only a faint whistle emerges. He shakes his head.

The other tribesmen, however, smile. One reaches for Gabriel's hand and lifts him to his feet. In the midst of the warriors, he is led into the village, welcomed.

Gabriel had discovered the *heart language* of the Guarani.

Each of us holds unique heart languages. These are the activities, symbols, or even objects in which we find special pleasure and delight.

Our words and ideas become incarnate when they are delivered in the heart language of another.

Sometimes, a heart language is a literal language—Russian, Mandarin, or Spanish. If you've ever seen the glow on the face of an immigrant who is addressed unexpectedly in her native tongue, you know how meaningful such incarnation can be.

Just as often, however, what is required to learn another's heart language is subtler than study of a foreign dialect.

Law enforcement experts working with youth gangs report that effective interaction with young gang members requires learning to speak their heart language: *respect.* If a street cop can learn to speak this "language," he will build rapport and gain respect for himself as well. Experts advise, for instance, never asking questions or dictating orders to a large group. Instead, inquire as to who is the gang's leader, and take him aside. Explain your concerns, and what you are asking him to do. More often than not, he will honor the request and bring the group into agreement also. Most of the other young men will value your decision to use their currency as well.

Perhaps more than anywhere else, heart languages are critical in expressing love.

Marriage counselor Dr. Gary Chapman has suggested that spouses, lovers, and friends use five distinct "love languages" to give and receive affection.[9] Each individual, he argues, experiences love most fully through only one of the five— either physical touch, gifts, quality time, affirmation, or acts of service. Typically, individuals attempt to convey love the way they like to receive it: through *their* own primary love language. But no matter how sincere, these efforts can fall flat. If we are to truly communicate love to another, concludes Dr. Chapman, we must learn to "speak" love to them using their primary language, rather than our own.

The fullest connections always require us to move beyond our own native language—learning to express through the heart language of others.

For Jesus, this included using phrases like "bread of life" (his audience's daily and most necessary staple) or "living water" (an image with rich symbolism in Jewish religion and also special poignancy in dusty Palestine). It also meant that his exchanges with a leper, blind man, or grieving widow would not turn first to issues of spiritual health, but to the pressing need felt by the person before him. Looking closely, we can see this use of others' heart languages in Jesus' choices of metaphors as well. Although he was a builder by trade, only a handful of Jesus' examples came from carpentry. Instead, the bulk were drawn from the daily labors of the farmers, fishermen, and homemakers who filled his audiences: fields ripe for harvest, fish being separated at the end of the day, or yeast in a batch of dough.

Today, this same decision may mean a husband learning to give gifts at unexpected times, even if he experiences love more fully through physical touch. For a parent, it might include becoming familiar with their teenager's favorite bands, despite the fact that Simon and Garfunkel really are the best ever. A heart language could involve a new sport or hobby, sign language, ethnic food, or old books. Whatever it may be, discovering another person's heart language—and learning to speak it—will incarnate our communication in their world like nothing else.

*   *   *   *

British statesman and financier Cecil Rhodes was known for his impeccable dress. One evening, a young man attending dinner at Rhodes' home arrived late. The fellow's train had just pulled into town, and, to his embarrassment, he had no chance to change his travel-stained clothes. Rhodes' other guests were already present, dressed with a precision worthy of their host.

Rhodes himself appeared later than expected. He was not dressed in impressive evening attire, but in a dingy old blue suit. Later, the young man later discovered that Rhodes had been about to welcome his guests in typical evening dress. But hearing of the young man's discomfort, he returned to his room and changed into the old suit.

Even more than learning and effort, the active ingredient in incarnation is gracious humility.

If our own image and priorities remain paramount, we will never take off our tuxedo and put on the old blue suit. Nor will we bother to learn the heart language of the Guarani, move to Molokai, or even spend the time necessary to really understand others. Pride will always seek to communicate from a position of power, distant and superior.

The best communicators, however, will always bend down and draw near, just as Jesus did when he wrapped a servant's towel around his waist and knelt to wash the feet of his students.

This bending low is not only for those whose position has put them "above" others. It can create connection for anyone, even those who find themselves at the bottom of the totem pole—the intern, the outsider. Regardless of status, every one of us delights to encounter an individual who cares enough about us to meet us where we are, who hazards the time and energy and risk it takes to come near, to be present with us and understand us, and to speak our language with sincerity.

The costs of this communication can be high. To connect with the Chinese, Hudson Taylor hazarded the loss of respect from Westerners, and even lower status in the eyes of many Chinese. Drawing near to wounded soldiers meant Clara Barton would not wait in safety for them to be brought to her. For Father Damien, taking on flesh among the lepers required leaving a comfortable church to live on Molokai; ultimately it cost him his life.

For Jesus, the costs were high as well. Because he entered homes and shared meals with tax collectors, prostitutes, and others of ill repute, the religious leaders derided him as a "friend of sinners." They slapped him with the labels "drunkard" and "glutton." Even Jesus' disciples were sometimes taken aback, like the time they found him at the town watering hole outside a Samaritan village, locked in conversation with a woman of dubious reputation.

But regardless of the risks, this was Jesus' way. As the Apostle Paul described, Jesus "made himself nothing, taking the very nature of a servant ... he humbled himself and became obedient to death, even death on a cross."

The risks will be real for us as well. Seeking to meet others on their turf and in their terms, we may be misunderstood. We will probably make mistakes, bumbling in a new language or culture. Our image may be compromised; others may think less of us. And the effort will almost certainly take far too much of our precious time.

But if we wish to connect—to *communicare*—there is no alternative.

*   *   *   *

In *Mortal Lessons: Notes on the Art of Surgery*, Dr. Richard Selzer described a scene he observed in a hospital room following an operation:

> I stand by the bed where a young woman lies, her face postoperative, her mouth twisted in a palsy, clownish. A tiny twig of a facial nerve, the one to the muscles of her mouth, has been severed. She will be thus from now on. The surgeon had followed with religious fervor the curve of her flesh; I promise you that. Nevertheless, to remove the tumor in her cheek, I had to cut the little nerve.
>
> Her husband is in the room. He stands on the opposite side of the bed, and together, they seem to dwell in the evening lamplight. Isolated from me, private. Who are they, I ask myself, he and this wry-mouth I have made, who gaze at each other, and touch each other generously, greedily?
>
> The young woman speaks. "Will I always be like this?" she asks. "Yes," I say. "It is because the nerve was cut." She nods and is silent. But the young man smiles. "I like it," he says. "It's kind of cute."
>
> All at once I know who he is. I understand, and I lower my gaze. One is not bold in an encounter with a god. Unmindful, he bends to kiss her crooked mouth, and I am so close I can see how he twists his own lips to accommodate hers, to show that their kiss still works. I remember that the gods appeared in ancient Greece as mortals, and I hold my breath and let the wonder in.

Yes, this is incarnation: conforming our lips to the distortions of another ... drawing near ... taking on flesh ... meeting on *their* turf and in *their* terms.

In every such act, real communication is born. Suddenly, we know—regardless of our differences and the vast gaps between us—we can still come together. We can kiss. And as we do, the electricity of life and thought, ideas and intimacy flows between us.

TAKE IT WITH YOU ...

In every interaction, pursue points of connection. This is where communication begins.

Don't fake it. Seek connection only as far as you sincerely desire to know and relate to another. If you must, settle for a connection that is less strong rather than pretend.

Take a moment to consider a relationship or two you desire to grow in the coming months. What are points of connection and commonality you can develop—through sharing experiences, honoring their culture, and self-disclosure? Is there a heart language you can learn to speak?

In a Media Age,
we assume that ...
When questions are asked,
we must deliver the right answers.

In Every Age,
the truth is ...
When you want to deliver the right answers,
ask good questions.

CHAPTER THREE

ASKING QUESTIONS:
How to Start a Revolution

How do revolutions begin?

Certainly, times of social tumult and radical change are frequently birthed with fiery rhetoric and booming calls to arms. In these often-bloody hours, every leader's sentence ends with an exclamation point.

But more often than not, look back a bit further, and you will find something else, something gentler and less emphatic, a symbol shaped as though it were bent over in humility and deference: the question mark.

Great communicators understand that well-formed questions can be wielded as a battle horn, soft and low at first, then growing as they echo from mind to heart and back again, serving as a clarion invitation to new possibilities and previously unconsidered truths.

Revolutions begin when someone asks a question.

A stumpy, toga-draped figure with a homely face is counted among the most influential men of all time.

Unlike the other great characters of ancient Athens, he chose to steer clear of politics and civic ladder climbing, and unlike other popular philosophers of his era, he wrote no books, established no school, and did not even offer any formal classes.

This man who has stood at the heart of Western philosophy for 2,400 years built his influence almost entirely upon conversations crafted with a single tool: the question.

Day in and day out, Socrates shaped the thoughts and perspectives of the students and others who gathered around him, drawing them with his questions toward new insights and perspectives:

"If a speech is to be good, must not the mind of the speaker know the truth about the matters of which he speaks?"

"But is it not better to be ridiculous than to be clever and an enemy?"

"[H]e who has learned what is just is just?"

The leading Athenians of Socrates' day had perhaps grown overly comfortable on slave labor, but they cannot be accused of being unperceptive. They knew that Socrates' unassuming dialogues and probing questions—what is today called the Socratic Method—presented more of a threat to Athens' status quo than even the enemy armies of mighty Sparta.

Despite his sincere piety and patriotism, Socrates was put on trial for subversion—corrupting the youth and undermining religious practices. A small majority of the jury voted to convict.

Rejecting their offer of life in exile, Socrates submitted to the jury's final sentence: death by suicide. He spent his final hours with students and family members. As the sun drew low in the Grecian sky, the aging teacher raised a cup of poisonous hemlock to his lips. He walked around the cell, allowing the poison to move into his bloodstream; then, as those gathered around him wept, he lay down, never to rise again.

His question-centered communication, however, continues

to reverberate. Athens, and with it the entire Western world, have never been the same.

*   *   *   *

Consider other great transformations in society: the fight for American independence. The invention of human flight. The struggle for civil rights and women's suffrage. The advent of radio and television. The explosion of the Internet.

All these "tipping points" in history started with questions— inquiries, second-guesses, an "is this the way things have to be?" that set in motion fundamental change.

Patrick Henry's patriotic challenge—"Is life so dear, or peace so sweet, as to be purchased at the price of chains and slavery?"—drew blacksmiths and bankers alike to risk all in a David-versus-Goliath battle for America's liberty.

The Suffragettes doggedly questioned why, if women were truly of the same value as men, they should not be allowed to vote. Ultimately, age-old conventions crumbled.

Martin Luther King, Jr.'s revolution was heavy with questions as well. If indeed "all men are created equal," why then should some be treated as more equal than others? Of those who wished to join him, Dr. King asked, "Are you able to accept blows without retaliating?" And of the complacent, King demanded, "[T]he question is not whether we will be extremists, but what kind of extremist we will be. Will we be extremists for hate or for love?"

Indeed, whatever the status quo may be, and no matter how smug, stifling, or self-satisfied it has become, it has no greater enemy than the question. Writing from behind the Iron Curtain in Soviet-dominated Czechoslovakia, Milan Kundera expressed, "...The true opponent of totalitarian kitsch [valueless culture] is the person who asks questions. A question is like a knife that slices through the stage backdrop and gives us a look at what lies hidden behind it."

Revolutionaries—those initiators of transformation in human lives—are men and women who understand the power of a question.

*　　*　　*　　*

Asking questions may not seem revolutionary at first glance. In fact, it often seems the opposite. To many, asking a question suggests lack of knowledge, uncertainty, even confusion. We assume powerful communicators deliver statements, assertions, and well-worded claims. They are continually declaring, alleging, pronouncing, affirming ... *anything* but asking.

And no wonder. Questions release control. They seem to place the listener in the driver's seat. And that, we often assume, is the death knell of effective communications.

Or is it?

"Once the question mark has arisen in the human brain the answer must be found, if it takes a hundred years. A thousand years."

—Jules Verne,
in *Journey to the Center of the Earth*[1]

Admittedly, modern communication is driven by assertions. Go there. Believe this. Buy those. Do that. Each day brings a fresh whirlwind of messages, each demanding that we alter yet another aspect of our beliefs and behaviors. These declarations are *answers*, bold and emphatic.

Cherry wood boardrooms and the marbled corridors of Capitol Hill rarely hear three simple words: *I don't know.* We are a culture ruled by answers and assertions. Deliberation is distrusted. Doubts are to be erased. Inquiry is suspicious.

But something remarkable happened to people when Jesus—the self-proclaimed answer—began asking questions.

*　　　*　　　*　　　*

The eyes of the religious rulers narrowed as they surveyed the scene before them. What gall for this Jesus to venture into their territory, the temple courts, teaching the gullible masses as if he had something the priests and theologians could not provide.

Clearly, the people were being mesmerized by the charlatan. The name of Jesus was on everyone's lips, from shopkeeper to centurion. There was danger of riots, even open revolt. It was all a little too much for those who valued stability, status, and tradition. For months the chief priests and elders had been watching and waiting, plotting, and biding their time.

Now here was the opportunity they'd been waiting for, a chance to force Jesus' hand. They paraded onto the scene, grand robes flowing out behind them, faces flushed with anger. How dare this troublemaker come here! They demanded an answer, once and for all.

A leading elder raised his voice, forcefully inquiring, "By what authority are you doing these things? And who gave you authority to do this?"

The rulers pursed their lips in satisfaction and rubbed their hands in delight. At last, this magician, this revolutionary, this fraud, would be exposed here—in the house of God—before hundreds of his followers and witnesses.

It was a good question. A mind-game. A trap. Just who had given him the right to make the bold claims he made? Jesus' answer would certainly expose him as a liar, or worse, a blasphemer—claiming to be the Son of God, an answer that would certainly incite the people against him.

Jesus knew he was being set up. He looked soberly around at the crowds hushed with anticipation, and nodded at the craftiness of the question. The rulers likely had spent many hours forming it.

"I will ask you one question," Jesus began. "Answer me, and I will tell you by what authority I am doing these things." The crowd gasped. The rulers' eyes narrowed, and their jaws clenched. Jesus continued. "John's baptism—was it from heaven, or from men?"

The old bearded men turned to one another. Whispers circulated the temple. Jesus had turned the tables. Instead of falling into the trap, he asked a question.

The rulers weighed their response, huddled together, gesturing, arguing in hushed tones. Answering that John the Baptizer had been nothing special would anger the crowd since the people viewed him as a prophet; but if the leaders affirmed John, they would implicate themselves for refusing to believe him, just as they were now doing with Jesus. Frustrated, and entangled in their own snare, they responded, "We don't know."

Jesus nodded. "Then neither will I tell you by what authority I am doing these things."

A murmur of delight rippled through the crowd. This rough-hewn carpenter had stymied the smug bluebloods again. And his *questions*—they seemed to have an answer imbedded in them as well. After all, John *was* a prophet anointed by heaven, the people knew that much for certain. And John *had* declared emphatically that Jesus was even greater than himself, the very "lamb of God who takes away the sin of the world." Could it be ...?

*　　　*　　　*　　　*

The Gospels, which record only a fraction of all Jesus said and did, contain more than one hundred fifty questions asked by Jesus. That's not exactly what you would expect from someone who claimed to be the answer.

The eighth chapter of Mark alone contains sixteen questions, each unique and piercing. They test faith, gently rebuke, explore the disciples' understanding of Jesus, and invite them to examine what they truly value.

Of course, Jesus was not one to shrink from controversial statements and bold assertions. But he also understood the profound power of the question.

Statements alone can be rigid, easily picked apart, and then disregarded in a debate over details. They tend to make demands of the audience rather than requests. They often give little space for the listener's own thought process, but instead try to orchestrate that process for them.

Jesus' questions, in contrast, invited others to participate in the activity of discovery, to take hold of truth for themselves. He understood that when an idea is imposed, however reasonable it might be, it is rarely held for long.

Consider some of Jesus' questions:

Who do you say that I am?

What do you want me to do for you?

Why do you call me good?

What were you arguing about on the road?

How many loaves do you have?

These are straightforward questions. Jesus may very well have known the answers ahead of time. Each one, however, goes deeper than might appear at first glance. It delves into murky corners where confusion, fear, and secrecy dwell, exposing them to the light of honesty, truth, and discovery.

Abraham Lincoln expressed well what we all intuitively know. If our attempts to motivate a person "dictate to his judgment, or to command his action," unless we wield some additional means of coercion, we will almost certainly meet with failure. "He will retreat within himself, close all the avenues to his head and his heart; and tho' your cause be naked truth itself ... you shall no more be able to [reach] him, than to penetrate the hard shell of a tortoise with a rye straw."[2]

Jesus' way stood in sharp contrast to a dictate-and-command approach. Instead, his questions invited listeners to embark on a search, candle in hand, rummaging through the attic of their minds for an adequate answer.

What often would be found in the process, Jesus knew, was the very instruction the individual most needed to hear: a truth known in childhood long buried in dust, the reality that they'd been living with a gap between their beliefs and actions, or a harmful attitude carelessly embraced. Within the ample space that questions allow, the searcher could ponder their discovery. In such a place, false assumptions and thoughtless habits could be exposed and found wanting.

Many of us are tempted to try to illuminate the way with a floodlight powered by our own blazing assertions. We want so badly to lead quickly and unambiguously to the answers we wish to provide. But *our* solution to the dimness might well have left those listeners blinded and recoiling, eyes shut tight against light for years. The candle, though perhaps through a slow and stumbling process, often achieves far more.

In this, we see that at the heart of Jesus' questions was a simple, driving purpose: *to prepare.* He sought to ready his listeners for something profound, something deep and satisfying, setting the stage for transformation.

It is impossible to force people to think or act or believe a certain way. Present all the right facts, have all the right answers, say all the right things, but the audience still might choose another path, buy the other product, or vote for the other candidate.

But effective communication can prepare your listeners. It removes obstacles, erects some signposts, and hands them a compass. The journey from thought to action, from ear to hand, from listening to responding is theirs. Your job is to help them along the way.

*   *   *   *

Nico Smith, like most Afrikaners of his era in South Africa, grew up drinking a doctrine of white superiority with his mother's milk. When the 1948 elections brought the Afrikaner Nationalists to power, nineteen-year-old Nico took to the streets to celebrate the arrival of government-sponsored apartheid.[3]

In his thirties, as an influential figure within the Dutch Reformed Church, Nico was recruited to join the elite fraternity known as the Broederbond. This group connected many of the most powerful members of society in a secretive brotherhood, working behind the scenes to advance the Afrikaner political and ideological agenda. These connections soon propelled Nico into a respected professorial position at Stellenbosch University.

> **PERSONAL NOTES—Jedd**
>
> John became a sort of mentor to me in college. He was a middle-aged man with a receding hairline, but you didn't notice it behind his jocular smile. We met every week or two for several years, digging together into things that mattered to me—faith, relationships, vocation, and the like.
>
> I remember distinctly the first time we got together, he asked questions for an hour and a half straight. Where I grew up. In what ways my parents influenced me. What places and activities I most loved. He listened to every response, and even took notes in a little brown notebook.
>
> As time went on, he offered thoughts and advice, too. But always, he returned to questions, listening carefully to my replies. I'd guess that in all our interactions, his questions outnumbered his suggestions two to one.
>
> It is difficult to say whether it was the questions themselves or the thoughts he shared in between them, but his impact still lingers deeply to this day. In terms of people I've spent the most time with over the years, John would probably not make the top one hundred. In terms of lasting influence, though, only a handful surpass him.

But on a visit to Switzerland in 1963, Nico met the great theologian Karl Barth. Near the end of his visit, Dr. Barth approached Nico and inquired politely, "May I ask you a personal question?" Nico nodded. He viewed conversing with the famed Christian thinker as a high privilege.

"Are you free to preach the Gospel in South Africa?" asked Barth.

"Yes, of course I am." Nico replied pleasantly. "Freedom of religion."

Barth shook his head. "That's not the kind of freedom I am asking about. Are you free in yourself? If you come across things in the Bible that are contrary to what your family and friends believe, will you preach it?"

Nico shrugged. "I've never come across something like that."

The elderly theologian would not be dissuaded. "Are you so free that even if you come across things in the Bible which are contrary to what your government is doing—that you will preach it?"

A crimson blotch rose on Nico's cheek, and he looked away. It was an awkward question, and he did not feel he had an adequate answer.

Nico was soon safely back in South Africa, but Barth's questions had somehow managed to travel with him. They lodged in his thoughts and stuck, like seed-carrying burrs caught in one's sock—not growing, but certainly not comfortable either.

It was a full ten years later at a meeting of the Broederbond that the revolution Barth had gently seeded finally took root. As Nico pondered the attitudes and actions of his associates, the answer to Barth's question sprang into his mind: I'm *not free!* He stood and walked out of the meeting.

Nico knew that quitting the Broederbond was social suicide.

At best, he could hope to step away without drawing much notice. He would live quietly, keeping a healthy separation between his newfound Christian convictions and political issues. For several years he did. But the questions would not be so easily satisfied.

When the government bulldozed a group of black squatter homes on the outskirts of town, some of Nico's students asked him what the Christian response should be. More questions. As he pondered the answer, he realized he could remain silent no longer. Nico drafted an official criticism of the government action and offered it for publication. There was now no going back.

A political firestorm began to envelope Nico. With little else to do, Nico sought guidance in prayer. As if in answer, the next Monday morning a telegram arrived from the black township of Mamelodi. The residents were asking that Nico become their pastor.

"God, no, I didn't ask for this," lamented Nico. Emotion surged over him, and he began to cry right in front of the postman. As he waited for his wife Ellen's return, Nico began to hope that she would reject the idea, giving him an easy out with God.

Ellen, however, provided him no excuses. "Nico, you realize that we'll have to go," she said after reading the telegram. The decision was made.

In the face of staggering social and even physical risks, Nico and Ellen left the university at Stellenbosch and filled the pastorship of the Mamelodi parish. Initially, they lived in a white suburb within driving distance of the township and commuted to the church. In time, however, they realized they could not truly minister to the people of Mamelodi without drawing nearer. A short while later, Nico and Ellen became the first whites under apartheid to receive official permission to live in a black area—the only white residents in a township of 300,000.

Nico and Ellen Smith's labors continue to bring healing to a torn nation. The seeds of their transformation were little more than a few simple questions.

*   *   *   *

There are many kinds of questions. Leading questions. Rhetorical questions. Condescending questions. Combative questions. Questions that are intended to obscure or instruct, insult or enlighten.

And while each distinct communication goal calls for its own unique questions, the best questions share a number of characteristics.

The questions Jesus asked were first of all *sincere*.

A question holds sincerity when the asker really cares what the listeners' response will be. That does not mean Jesus never sensed what reply he would be given, or never sought to guide discussion toward particular conclusions. It is just that what his listener's thought and felt really mattered to him—and that is why he asked, not just to confuse them or make a point or demonstrate his own cleverness.

Jesus' questions were always *attuned to the uniqueness of each situation*.

Effective question-asking requires a sensitivity to what is occurring at the moment, and also to the readiness of others to receive the questions. As discussed in chapter one, genuine attentiveness is a critical part of honing effective, fitting inquiries.

Jesus consistently did this. His questions mixed naturally with the discussion at hand, frequently flowing out of the events unfolding at the time: a dispute among his disciples, a hungry crowd, or a verbal attack from the religious authorities. Quite often, his questions were directed at subtle attitudes or sub-plots that most busy people would not even have noticed. Questions fitted to the experiences and emotion of specific circumstances yield the best results.

Jesus' questions were *fit to the audience.*

Each one showed a deep awareness and thorough consideration of the audience's beliefs and biases, background and assumptions, fears and priorities.

Take, for instance, the story we call "The Good Samaritan," a phrase Jesus' audience would have considered an oxymoron. From the Jewish perspective, this parable painted a shocking image: a despised, half-breed heretic whose active concern for a crime victim surpassed that of two Jewish holy men. Rather than conclude with a pithy instruction, Jesus finished with a question, "Which of the three was the true neighbor?"

No doubt, many in the audience writhed internally at the notion that a filthy Samaritan could be considered a protagonist. Yet still, the prickly truth could hardly be avoided: True neighbor love is not based on race or group identity, but upon a decision to serve. Jesus' question served as a crowbar, perfectly fitted to the task of breaking apart centuries-old prejudices and faulty assumptions about the limits of loving one's neighbor.

Jesus' questions were also *decisively clarifying.*

They penetrated to the heart of the matter, peeling back layer after layer of what *appeared* to be the real issue so as to address what actually *was* the real issue.

"What good is it for a man to gain the whole world and lose his soul?" posed Jesus. A question like this forces self-scrutiny, a rethinking of priorities, and ultimately, a critical decision. Will temporary, external things like possessions and status continue to dominate life? Or will there be a reorientation of energies toward matters of eternal significance—seeking God and serving neighbors?

As theologian Hans Küng observed, despite Jesus' welcoming invitation to all, his claims, questions, and even actions consistently "confronted people with a final decision. Jesus left no one neutral. He himself had become the great question."[4]

Finally, Jesus' questions *provided space for the audience to decide.*

Despite his passion for truth, Jesus' communication was not manipulative or coercive. He never pushed for the hard sell.

Whether using questions or not, Jesus consistently left room for his listeners' decision-making process. Nearing his death in prison, John the Baptist sent to ask one last time, just to be sure, if Jesus was indeed the Messiah. Jesus did not respond with a criticism of doubt, nor did he provide an exclamation point affirmation. He simply instructed the messenger to describe to John what he had observed: lame beggars leaping for joy, a once-sightless grandmother tracing clouds with her fingertip, a deaf little girl tapping her feet to a tune. The conclusion John would have to draw for himself.

This non-coercive, put-the-ball-in-their-court approach flies in the face of a "close the deal ASAP" mentality. It places itself at the mercy of the listener, and her unpredictable and slower-than-ideal processing. When a quick sale is your only measure of success, you'd do best to resort to other methods. But whenever long term buy-in or enduring life change is the goal, there is simply no substitute for questions that are sincere, situation-specific, audience centered, and decisively clarifying, and that allow your listeners to decide for themselves.

*   *   *   *

Few grasped this principle better than a member of the British Parliament named William Wilberforce.

In 1787, the heart of this twenty-eight-year-old political protégé was ignited by a spiritual awakening. Being "Christian" in name only would no longer be enough. He would live as an apprentice to Jesus, or nothing at all.

Wilberforce initially considered abandoning his auspicious career in Parliament for the pulpit. Former slave trader John Newton urged young William not to leave his position, but instead to offer God his political talents. Wilberforce agreed, and committed to using his energies for God's purposes for as long as he would remain in public office.

Soon after, Wilberforce was gripped by a sense of calling to two principal goals, and he resolutely penned in his journal, "God Almighty has set before me two great objects, the suppression of the Slave Trade and the reformation of manners [morals]."

This young statesman would be shooting for the moon. No serious politician dared take on slavery, the lucrative centerpiece of the British economy, and only a fool would hope to remain in office by challenging the moral choices of the elite. His first attempt at abolishing the slave trade received only one vote in Parliament: his own.

Wilberforce was not deterred. Armed with a squeaky voice and a slight build, he spent the next forty years introducing resolutions in Parliament, gathering like-minded leaders, drafting pamphlets, and winsomely urging others to reconsider their assumptions. Alongside small victories came harassment, hardship, and even violence.

Among Wilberforce's central tactics, often overlooked, was his use of questions, or "launchers," as he called them.

As a political leader, he interacted daily with the trendsetters and opinion leaders of Britain. Before arriving at a social event or dinner party, he always spent at least a few moments thinking about the hosts and guests, writing down questions that might direct conversations toward higher purposes and deeper thinking. He sought to develop the kind of questions that would "launch" conversations into areas of morality, faith, and cultural values—everything from marital fidelity to the scourge of slavery.

Wilberforce's questions steered hearts and minds toward truths that many were normally unwilling or unprepared to discuss. Through the conversations that flowed from these relevant and personal questions, a great many leaders were challenged to rethink long-held assumptions about slavery and the social order of the day.

It was not until Wilberforce lay stretched on his deathbed that the joyous news was delivered: Parliament had voted to abolish the trafficking of slaves. Meanwhile, his efforts to inspire virtue helped usher in an era of fresh moral clarity and new-found concern for the downtrodden and needy.

Wilberforce, and his questions, had turned British society on its head.

*　　　*　　　*　　　*

Approached in Jesus' way, communication is always about the audience, whether a single friend or crowded room. We sometimes forget that. Questions are one sure means of turning the focus back where it belongs—on the people with whom we desire to connect.

By asking questions, we *honor* the listener, conveying a respect for her autonomy and a trust in her ability to choose. When the question is asked and the communicator pauses, suddenly the listener is once again the focal point. A faint spark of pleasure passes through her as she realizes her thoughts matter and her opinion is valued. In this way, question-asking is an inherently subversive activity.

Our culture tacitly affirms that what I want and what I think is supreme. We know we ought to care about others too, of course, but always about ourselves first. The word "me" stands at the middle of every equation. Even those of us who imagine ourselves good listeners, if the truth be told, spend the bulk of every conversation thinking—if not speaking—about our own interests and concerns. Question-asking slashes against this status quo. It places *the other* at the center point, undermining the corrosive institution of self-centeredness.

Admittedly, honoring listeners with questions carries hazards. We may lose an element of control as they become involved in the learning process. But the truth is that we never really had control in the first place. In the final analysis, even our best attempts to impact and influence must end with the listeners deciding for themselves.

Questions simply lead toward those crucial decisions. By its

PERSONAL NOTES—Erik

I knew it would be a tedious conversation the moment I met the man. He had a U-turn way of conversing—stories and statements that always came back to him, to his achievements, to his views on life. It is like what I was telling my friend in the music business ... You have to agree with what I am saying ... If I ever had the ear of the president ...

I strained to get the attention of a friend who could rescue me. I proceeded with the typical conversation-closers. "That's great. Well, we're about to hit the road ..." Nothing seemed to work. He was desperate for attention, almost begging to be known.

Reluctantly, I admit to my shame, I began to ask some questions, each one a bit more probing—and sincere—than the last. How did your wife handle the move? You dream of becoming a writer? So your father passed away when you were in high school? The conversation slipped from the safe shorelines into something deeper. He became animated with new stories and new revelations. Our conversation was interrupted a short time later. He nodded, and we went our separate ways. I have not seen him since. I don't think he knows much more than my name, but I know a lot about him. A few weeks ago, I ran into a mutual friend, and the conversation turned to this guy. "He said he really liked talking with you. I heard the two of you had a good conversation," my friend related. Conversation? Not exactly. He did most of the talking. Connection? Absolutely.

very nature, a question evokes an almost irresistible response. It invites hearers to places they may have never ventured before—places where they can scrutinize life from unexpected vantage points, rethink deeply rooted assumptions, and probe unexamined motives and values.

In short, questions draw others to places where new answers can be found.

Insights encountered along this route do not feel to the learner like they have been somehow foisted upon them. The new truths have been *personally identified* rather than dictated by someone else, *discovered* rather than prescribed. And while ideas pushed on us from the outside tend to remain on the surface of our lives, beaded up like water droplets on a sealed deck, answers we arrive at "on our own" begin almost immediately to sink deep, reshaping our behaviors and thoughts at the deepest level.

That is why self-discovered truths are always far more powerful and enduring than those that are imposed or spoon-fed. They inevitably penetrate deeper, reside longer, and influence more thoroughly. Often, they will continue to impact for a lifetime.

If you want to make a statement, ask questions.

If you want to convince, ask questions.

If you want to honor your listeners, ask questions.

If you want to change hearts and minds for the long haul, ask questions.

And the better the questions, the more remarkable the result.

TAKE IT WITH YOU ...

We live in an exclamation culture—where bold claims and boisterous assertions and are the currency of attention and influence. Use questions to subvert the status quo and seed mini-revolutions.

Don't expect good questions to appear from nowhere. Spend a few moments, even before casual social interactions, considering questions you can ask. You'll be surprised at what follows.

Great communicators, like Jesus, understand the power of questions—to turn the message back to the listeners and invite them to discover truth for themselves. Make learning the skill of question-asking a top priority in the growth of your communication.

Make a list of questions that lead to open-ended conversation. Surprise the listener with unexpected inquiries. Try replacing, "What work do you do?" with "What work *would* you do if you could do anything you wanted?"

As an occasional exercise, try going for five minutes in a conversation without making a single statement, only asking questions.

In a Media Age,
we assume that ...
Image sells, and spin saves.

In Every Age,
the truth is ...
People crave authenticity.

CHAPTER FOUR

AUTHENTICITY:
A Draught of the Real

The convention hall was a pinwheel of words and color. In front of the bunting-decked stage, an ensemble of musicians bounced to their own patriotic tunes. Homemade signs littered the walls. Political delegates, engaged in last-minute deals and debates, awaited the next speech.

The crowd applauded respectfully as another candidate approached the podium. His tailored suit and gel-locked hair were perhaps a touch out of place in the middle-class town, host to a northwest state's political convention.

The candidate removed his glasses, slowly, thoughtfully, then began his speech. The words were precise, the gestures powerful. His baritone voice rose and fell at exactly the right moments.

The crowd, however, hardly responded. They sat disinterested, arms crossed, heads cocked back in suspicion.

Why?

Commentators agreed he had offered the right words, the right gestures and tone and look. The listeners, however, seemed to sense that something was just not quite right. "It was too perfect," said some.

And they were right. A news story later reported that the candidate's text—inadvertently distributed to a reporter—included reminders to "lift glasses here and look sincere" and "pound podium" and other instructions for making his speech appear genuine. The words had indeed been skillfully written and delivered, but they apparently reflected little from the candidate's heart. The crowd refused to buy it.

*   *   *   *

Whatever else may be said of people today, it is safe to assume they are thirsty. Most of us are, feeling parch-mouthed for just a few refreshing droplets of something real, lasting, and true.

Indeed, we long for *authenticity*.

American industry, even with its awe-inspiring production of consumer goods, seems utterly incapable of mass-fabricating this commodity. Amid increasingly desperate attempts, the best our entertainment and commercial sectors can supply are all-too-unreal "reality shows" and an endless stream of products carefully manufactured by the thousands to appear one-of-a-kind.

And so we wander in a desert of spin, hype, and well-manicured impressions. From the mirages painted by advertising to the etched-in-stone smile of the woman in the pew next to us, almost everything we are asked to swallow tastes more like dust than water.

But the oasis may lie closer than we think.

Communication often obscures as much as it reveals. Whether intentionally or not, it warps and conceals the underlying reality being conveyed, and delivers instead a doctored image or made-for-consumption impression. Authentic communicators cut in the opposite direction. They strive to allow others to see and encounter things as they are.

It is this *encounter with the real* that can give our communication that rare, thirst-slaking quality most people are panting for: authenticity.

*　　*　　*　　*

The pious clergyman stood at his favorite spot in the temple courtyard for prayer, just far enough from the gate to be unobtrusive but easily noticed. People needed to see a good example, he knew. His silvering hair appeared dry and tangled—he had not run any oil through it today, a clear indication that he was again fasting. His eyes swept the courtyard, narrowing slightly as he caught sight of one of those insufferable tax collectors huddled in the far corner.

Raising his face to the sky, the clergyman began, words well enunciated, just loud enough for passersby to hear—"I thank you, God. Yes, I *thank* you. I am no thief, no doer of injustice, no thinker of lustful thoughts. I am nothing like such men. Twice a week, I go without eating so I can devote myself to prayer. I faithfully give generously of my wealth to you. Yes, I thank you."

His eyes closed for a blissful moment as he finished. He then began toward the exit, slowly. Beneath his beard, a smile played upon his lips. He could feel admiring eyes upon his back.

The tax collector, meanwhile, had not noticed the clergyman's prayer. A short distance away, he bent low, his lips pressed hard against a clinched hand. An anguished sigh slipped from his lips. He knew his guilt—bribing officials, extorting extra fees from business owners, even squeezing pennies out of the widows. Oh, how he now desired to change! What could he say? He choked back the tears, finally stuttering, "Have mercy

... on me, God ... a sinner." The sun was casting long shadows when he finally rose. No one seemed to observe as he passed quickly from the courtyard, his eyes moist and bright with relief.

In this parable told by Jesus, the clergyman's prayer left the primary audience, God, thoroughly unimpressed. Even if his behavior was as spotless as he let on, his pride and smug self-satisfaction soured it all. The tax collector's simple words, however, were different. Despite his past failings and inarticulate sputtering, God received the humble, heartfelt honesty with gracious welcome.

God is not the only one who feels this way, it seems. For most of us, presentations that smack of self-importance or insincerity, even if impeccably delivered, produce little but annoyance. In contrast, words flowing from the heart in humble honesty can hardly help but elicit warmth and interest.

> "The weight of this sad time we must obey. Speak what we feel, not what we ought to say."
>
> —Edgar, at the tragic end of *King Lear*

For most of us, just a pinch of heart-and-soul can outweigh a boatload of Toastmasters' savvy.

This is not to say that transparency in communication is the only thing that matters. Attire, vocabulary, diction, and other elements of presentation are important factors in communication, and there is no reason to neglect them. Possession of real skills and knowledge is vital as well. After all, just about anyone would prefer that a skilled surgeon, even an arrogant one, slice into their sternum rather than a well-meaning banker. Even so, something draws the deeper part of us almost irresistibly to the ragged-edged real, even over the sleek, smooth, and stunning.

Deep down, most of us know quite well that our influence will be tepid and our relationships shallow if we consistently shy away from authenticity in our communication. So then why is it so rare?

Very simply, because we fear.

We fear the deflation of our image and diminishment in the eyes of those who respect us. We fear rejection. We fear we will undermine the causes we believe in or the faith we want others to embrace. We fear our longings will be mocked and our dreams dismissed. We fear followers will no longer follow, students will no longer listen, and admirers will no longer admire.

And so we remain no more transparent than canal water, revealing a shadowed outline here or there, but leaving our deeper thoughts, fears, failings, and hopes hidden beneath the murk.

John Eldredge sums it up well in *Wild at Heart*, comparing the way we veil our true selves to how Adam and Eve concealed themselves behind the foliage in the Garden of Eden: "We are hiding, every last one of us. Well aware that we, too, are not what we were meant to be, desperately afraid of exposure, terrified of being seen for what we are and are not, we have run off into the bushes. We hide in our office, at the gym, behind the newspaper and mostly *behind our personality*. Most of what you encounter when you meet a man is a façade, an elaborate fig leaf, a brilliant disguise."[1]

Certainly, most of us readily affirm that "everyone is human." We allow ourselves excuses, explanations, and plenty of grace—often far more than we allot to others. But in our communication, from casual greetings to small group settings to public speaking, we shy away from revealing any but the most innocuous imperfections.

It is not hard to see why we feel our persona must be nearly flawless. After all, everyone else is, it seems—at least, everyone who matters.

Consider the fact that for every alluring photo included in *Sport's Illustrated*'s yearly swimsuit edition, roughly twenty-five thousand photographs are taken and discarded. And that is *after* starting with statuesque models who likely have undergone intense dieting, rigorous exercise, and scores of cosmetic surgeries—not to mention the lights, make-up, and exotic settings. Tragically, countless women hold such photos as the standard for beauty, with devastating consequences for their health, confidence, and sense of priorities.

Of course, beauty is not the only measuring stick. We are just as easily drawn toward elusive ideals in professional success, popularity, articulate speech, or general having-it-all-togetherness. If we wish to influence or even be accepted by others, we feel we had best keep our all too real shortcomings submerged.

But what type of person influences you? Only the flawless? What is it that draws you up on your tiptoes to listen? What tugs not just your eyes, but also your heart? Certainly, carefully-crafted images of beauty, power, and success are alluring. But do they leave lasting impact, or merely fade as quickly as they are replaced?

The truth is, at the first whiff of something real, people come running.

*   *   *   *

Jesus was thoroughly real. Unlike many skilled communicators, his words and presentation were never delivered as a smoke-screen to obscure his true thoughts or character. He wove his very self into his communication, presenting not only concepts and instructions, but his personhood, as he truly was.

Again and again, this startling approach cowed his enemies and stirred the crowds to awe.

Three qualities in particular made Jesus' communication authentic.

First, Jesus exhibited extraordinary vulnerability.

It would be hard to find a greater contrast than Jesus to today's model communicator: slick, polished, and unflappable, glimmering smiles with whitened teeth. Jesus made no attempt to bury the messy edges of life and tangled emotions that most of us keep carefully tucked away in our back pockets. Distress and elation, dependence and affection, anguish and need were all threads within Jesus' communication—just as they form the fabric of life.

When students Jesus had sent out returned glowing with success, Jesus gushed with thankfulness to God. Facing a band of arrogant clergy, his face darkened with frustration, marked by distress from their indifference to human suffering. When many of his followers were abandoning him, Jesus turned to the disciples, his words gentle and exposed: "You, too, will not leave me, will you?" he asked. Arriving in Jerusalem to the songs of adoring crowds, Jesus wept in their midst at the hard-heartedness that had marked the people of David's city in every generation. Again and again, Jesus' disciples wondered at his overflowing tenderness toward the hapless masses.

Even as he sensed his death approaching, Jesus did not grow stoic or distant, as one might expect. Despite his steely determination, he bore his heart to his friends and begged them to remain near. "My soul is overwhelmed with sorrow to the point of death. Stay here and keep watch with me."

From first to last, Jesus allowed his true self to radiate through his communication—even those elements that might seem to diminish stature or nobility. This vulnerability did not dull his impact or blunt his influence; it only made them brighter and sharper.

Second, Jesus spoke with a startling forthrightness.

It is easy to imagine Jesus as the Sunday school cutout figure, smiling demurely with a lamb slung over his shoulders. And no wonder. Bright-eyed children delighted in Jesus' presence, and his companions marveled at the grace and mercy conveyed by his presence.

Even so, Jesus did not hesitate to deliver hard words that needed to be heard. His language could strike like brass knuckles when necessary—condemning injustice, exposing deceptive half-truths, or confronting double standards.

Significantly, Jesus directed his harshest words toward those who embodied the *opposite* of authenticity. To the strutting theologians who disguised their flaws behind façades of perfection, Jesus gave the label hypocrites—literally, "actors." He took a sledgehammer to their stony hearts. "You are blind guides," he declared. "A brood of vipers." "White-washed tombs full of dead men's bones."

Jesus did not attempt to soft sell the life he was offering either. Today, effective car salespersons turn prospective buyers' focus away from costs and onto benefits—"Just imagine how good it will feel to get behind the wheel ..." Jesus did the opposite. If you buy what I am selling, he warned, it will involve daily self-denial; consider the cost carefully before you begin.

Of course, Jesus was capable of remarkable tact, and his words consistently conveyed sincere love and a deep sense of grace. Whatever the message, though, Jesus never abandoned forthrightness.

Third, Jesus made himself surprisingly accessible.

Conventional wisdom notes that familiarity breeds contempt. Those who wish to be revered, therefore, make their appearances short and tightly controlled. Many celebrities, politicians, and circuit speakers operate with the same basic plan: Deliver what you have to say, shake a few hands, and then head for the door.

Jesus' approach could not have been more different. He made his place continually *with* the people, walking their streets, teaching on familiar hillsides and lakeshores, sharing meals in their homes. Children crawled up into his lap, the sick grasped at his clothing, a prostitute washed his feet in her tears.

Jesus made himself even more starkly available to his primary students. As the Gospel of Mark describes, he set apart twelve disciples for the primary purpose "that they might *be with him*." And they were, continuously—traveling, eating, sleeping, struggling, celebrating—always together. As professor Robert Coleman noted in his insightful study of Jesus' teaching methods, "Amazing as it may seem, all Jesus did to teach these men his way was to draw them close to himself. He was his own school and curriculum ... Knowledge was not communicated by the Master in terms of laws and dogmas, but in the living personality of One who walked among them."[2]

> **"We glide past each other ... because we never dare to give ourselves."**
>
> —Dag Hammarskjold[3]

The consistent authenticity of Jesus' communication was not lost on his disciples. Years down the road, as Matthew, John, Peter, and others helped put the accounts of their experiences with Jesus into written form, they embraced the same principle.

It would have been tempting to do otherwise. After all, these men had by now become esteemed leaders of the burgeoning community of Christian believers. One could easily have argued that the success of the movement depended heavily upon careful cultivation of their reputation and status.

Like their master, they chose vulnerable truth-telling over burnished image.

The disciples, as presented by their own writings, are anything but winsome heroes shining with wisdom and virtue. In fact, the Gospels portray their authors as just the opposite: painfully unperceptive and slow to learn, feeble in faith, given to superstition and fear, continually asking dull questions and expressing timid doubts, and scattering at the first hints of danger.

Virtually every page of the Gospels contains poignant examples of the disciples' shortcomings. The rag-tag band seems to forget with almost comic regularity lessons learned just days before. Even at their final meal with Jesus, they squabble over who would be the greatest among them. As their teacher sweats blood in anticipation of his death, they fall asleep, just yards away. When a band of brigands arrives to arrest him, they disappear into the darkness, some denying they ever knew him.

Describing their experiences with Jesus, these men faithfully offer readers of the Gospels nothing less than an *encounter with the real*. They present themselves not as towers of virtue or saintly heroes, but as they really were: an oddball collection of stragglers, doubters, and screw-ups whom Jesus chose to embrace.

Yet this authenticity did not diminish their ability to communicate with power. If anything, it only increased it. And the books they wrote? They are the most-read texts of all time.

*   *   *   *

Samuel Taylor Coleridge's famous tale, "The Rime of the Ancient Mariner," describes sailors dying of thirst, languishing on a stranded ship in windless seas, battered by a merciless sun. The poem's most famous line—"water, water everywhere, [but not a] drop to drink,"—depicts much of modern communication and culture.[4] All around are vast seas of promised refreshment, but it seems the deeper we drink of them, the thirstier we grow.

But like soft rain on our ship's sun-brittled deck, authentic communication brings health and new life in the most delightful ways.

Its first gift is the healing of reconciliation.

No matter how well articulated, words inevitably arrive stillborn when delivered into an environment of suspicion, anger, fear, or bitterness. In such circumstances, to speak the whole truth with authenticity is often the first and most necessary balm.

Tom Tarrants, who now serves as the director of the respected C.S. Lewis Institute, was once feared across America as a terrorist with the White Knights of the Ku Klux Klan. His crimes, particularly violence against African-Americans, inscribed his name on the FBI's most wanted list.

When asked if African-Americans are willing to receive him, Tarrants shared that he often feels more welcomed by the black community than anywhere else. Why? He explains that when he speaks, he always comes clean with his past bigotry and the wrongs he has done. In a community that often feels a subtle racism from even the most "enlightened" whites, Tarrants' openness about matters that usually remain beneath the surface is a salve to deep wounds—enabling forgiveness and reconciliation to begin. Authenticity is always the first step in healing.

Authenticity's second gift, trust, is always in need.

Public trust seems to slide ever lower, driven by the never-ending parade of baseless advertising claims, campaign mudslinging, pedophile priests, and corporate scandals. The results of a *New York Times*/CBS News poll showed nearly two-thirds of respondents believed that in dealing with "most people," you simply "can't be too careful."[5]

PERSONAL NOTES—Jedd

Three close friends and I wrote the book *Four Souls* together, sharing the tales of our seven-month journey around the globe, living and working in countries from Guatemala to Vietnam.

Our intent was to write with transparency, holding nothing back. Along with our brighter and braver moments, we would lay bare our blunders, quarrels, and insecurities.

Our authenticity in the book, I see now, was only partial. As much as we desired to communicate with transparency, our own subtle inclination toward preserving image remained tenacious. Deep down, know I wanted to be transparent, but perhaps not to the extent that readers would think less of me.

Despite this, some of the stories did come through with authenticity, stripped of the varnish we would have liked to leave in place. As a result, many readers have expressed finding a sense of deep connection in reading the book.

What has struck me most is that rarely do readers mention the accounts that portray the moments of which I am most proud. The connection most often seems to have been found in regard to weaker moments—the stories I would have preferred to leave out: unsettling doubts in my faith, a puppy-love crush I had on a Russian girl, or a selfish conflict over which route we would take. The places of greatest vulnerability, it seems, are often the places of greatest connection.

Interestingly, the same study also showed that the respondents believed that of the people they "know personally," a full 85 percent would "try to be fair." Other studies reveal a similar reality. When people feel that they know us, they are much more likely to view us as honest, fair, and well intentioned. By opening our lives and inviting others in, authentic communication builds a sense of personal knowledge and familiarity and establishes a foundation for trust.

This trust only increases as it becomes clear that our words too are authentic.

Authentic communication goes beyond merely avoiding lies. Communication becomes authentic as it reveals the *whole* truth—awkward, vulnerable, and inconvenient as it may be. It is a homeseller disclosing an issue no one would have noticed, a researcher pointing out potential flaws in her findings, an apologist for the faith acknowledging questions he doesn't know how to answer. Choosing this path builds trust and adds a weight to our words that no mere technique could ever buy.

In a tribute to professor Neil Postman, a former student attributed Postman's fabled effectiveness as a teacher to this sort of authenticity. Although his reputation as a thinker was legend, Postman made his claims with an authentic humility, always "acknowledge[ing] the possibility that he may be mistaken." This, noted the student, "was the essence of what made him such a great force in teaching. He felt things strongly, and articulated them wisely—often with a wink and a smile—but was always willing to concede the possibility that his feelings were stronger than his facts, which made us all the more likely to agree with him ..."

Authenticity presents our messy situations, flawed selves, and fallible conclusions as they really are—messy, flawed, and fallible—building confidence and trust like nothing else.

Upon trust, authenticity builds toward its highest blessing: the rich kinship of intimacy.

It seems we have nothing in common with certain people. Such thoughts are always mistaken. The realm of our shared experience is far larger than eyes could ever discern.

This common territory is especially found in our weaknesses and aspirations, failure and hope, fear and passion. When we have the courage to venture into that land as communicators, we inevitably find our hearers already there, ahead of us. When spoken with authenticity, our words express what others have often thought and felt, but not dared to express.

In the book *A Severe Mercy*, writer Sheldon Vanauken offers a breathtakingly transparent look into his own heart and the story of his romance, love, and ultimate loss to cancer of his wife Davy. He allows the reader to gaze in upon his deepest hopes and anguish, failures and pride, desperate love and tragic loss.

Vanauken reported that soon after his book was published, the flood of letters, phone calls, and visitors began. Many readers expressed feeling as if they and they alone had been penetrated to the depths of their being. They sensed that a deep and mysterious kinship had grown between themselves and the author. Vanauken agreed, but reminded them that the kinship they felt was much broader than any of them knew.

He explained, "It is, I think, that we are all so alone in what lies deepest in our souls, so unable to find the words and perhaps the courage to speak with unlocked hearts, that we do not know at all that it is the same with others. And since I had been compelled, somewhat reluctantly, to go beyond reticence, readers were moved to kinship with one they felt to be the only other being who also knew."[6]

Those who are committed to authentic communication consistently *give names* to the feelings, sensations, and experiences others have known but have never uttered. Inevitably, such communication touches both hearts and minds, knitting us to others with an intimacy we have never before experienced.

The quest to become authentic communicators is not as simple as some imagine. Cheap imitations abound. Bona fide authenticity is not attained merely by throwing off restraint— belching up crass "unmentionables," verbally streaking, or grasping for unearned intimacy by emptying our souls in a first encounter. Such approaches may be stimulating, but they do not take us to places of common ground, trust, and mutual respect. There are times, also, when biting one's tongue is simply the higher path. Should not a father sometimes swallow his fears for the benefit of his children? And how long can you stand to be around a whiner who remains steadfastly "authentic" with her every gripe?

Clearly, authentic communication requires discernment.

Like most pathways worth taking, it also involves a repeated choosing. Four decisions, in particular, confront us daily. Each response either shapes us into increasingly authentic communicators ... or leads in the opposite direction.

1. *The decision to prize truth-telling over image-making.*

Russian dissident Alexander Solzhenitsyn experienced first-hand the horror of Joseph Stalin's murder of millions of Soviet citizens. He spent years behind the razor wire of Siberian prison camps, and his family and close friends numbered among the dead. Yet looking back upon this evil, Solzhenitsyn declared that if placed in a situation identical to Stalin's, he may well have carried out the same atrocities. Pointing to himself he acknowledged, "The line dividing good and evil cuts through the heart of every human being."[7]

If we're honest with ourselves, we too know the vastly divergent qualities inhabiting every heart, including our own—good and evil, certainty and doubt, humility and ego, compassion and apathy. As French mathematician and thinker Blaise Pascal observed in his *Pensees*, each one of us is marked by both wretchedness and greatness; at the same time, we are both angel and beast. Our world is equally bi-polar. It is full of dancing fireflies, grandmother's kisses, and peaceful Sunday afternoons ... but also car accidents, Alzheimer's disease, and disintegrating marriages.

If we refuse to acknowledge *both* sides of this reality, we will inevitably abandon truthfulness, somehow imagining that a brushed-up picture will accomplish more than unvarnished truth.

Of course, it is easy for us to nod in affirmation of truth-telling. Still, we must beware: The lies we are most tempted to tell are not statements that could be proven false in a courtroom. They are subtler, usually sufficiently so to fool the one telling them—faint shadings, slight distortions, and positive "spin." Justifying ourselves, we point out that we did not speak the half-truths to benefit ourselves, but to help the good cause advance, the company expand, or the faith be embraced.

Great communicators choose a different path. From St. Augustine and Leo Tolstoy to Joni Eareckson Tada, Philip Yancey and Bono, their words carry a penetrating honesty about the world and themselves, glistening with both beauty and brokenness. The same is true of the pastor who speaks forthrightly about his experience of doubt or struggle, or the principal who shares with her students the painful consequences of mistakes she made at their age.

If we desire to become such communicators, says writer Frederick Buechner, we must "use words and images that help make the surface of our lives transparent to the truth that lies deep within ... speaking forth not only the light and the hope of it but the darkness as well."[8] If we are brave enough to tell this deeper truth, Buechner assures, we will "set echoes going the way a choir in a great cathedral does."[9]

2. *The decision to build character rather than manage impressions.*

Dr. Stephen Covey made a remarkable discovery in his landmark research into American success literature written from 1776 to 1976.[10] For the first 150 years, the literature emphasized development of character and abilities as the sure path to success. Covey labeled this approach the *character ethic.* The subsequent fifty years of success literature, in contrast, focused heavily on the use of surface level techniques and personality skills to portray a successful image—whether or not this image coincided with underlying reality. Covey called this the *personality ethic.* More recently, he has noted that despite lip service to the contrary, this focus on image and personality has become even more pronounced over the past twenty-five years.

The personality ethic, especially relating to communication, is hard to resist. Everyone wants to be well-received. We desire to leave audiences impressed, if only the small circle of friends at the dinner party. The personality ethic is the easy way, requiring only cosmetic self-improvement and easily attained skills.

Character is the harder road. Impression settles for a quick coat of cheerful paint; the character-builder repairs dry rot with lumber, nails, and sweat. Impression seeks a slim waist using diet pills and a cinched-up corset; the character-builder relies on exercise and vegetables.

In the end, the way of the character-builder is the only route to the integrity Jesus possessed—a *oneness* between what lay within and what others saw. This kind of integrity permits no gap between *persona* and true self, nor does it allow cultivation of an image that does not reflect deeper reality. Its hope is simple, in the words of Plato: "May the inner and the outer person meet."

3. *The decision to offer what you have, rather than what you wish you could give.*

An expansive collection of studies from 2001 to 2003 by the Gallup organization gave piercing examination to thousands of businesses worldwide.[11] At the heart of the research was the driving question, *What makes successful companies successful?*

In response, it became clear that one primary factor separates the most effective enterprises from the rest of the pack: their response to employees' strengths and weaknesses. Mediocre companies tend to focus on "fixing" employees' deficiencies so workers will better fit their job descriptions. In contrast, superior businesses focus on strengths, cultivating each employee's natural abilities and building job descriptions around an individual's unique gifts. Over time, the review concluded, the first route leads to sub-par outcomes, the second to envied success.

We face this crossroad in our own communication as well. Dwelling on our shortcomings or trying to fake strengths we imagine others expect of us will lead to uninspiring results. In contrast, communicators who employ their natural talents, however modest, rarely fail to leave an impact.

The great composer, Beethoven, was not known for social grace. Being deaf, he found conversation difficult and even humiliating. When he heard of the death of a friend's son, Beethoven hurried to the house, overcome with grief. He had no words of comfort to offer, but there in the room he found a piano. For the next half hour he played, pouring out his emotions in the most eloquent way he could. When he finished playing, he left. The friend later remarked that no one else's visit had meant so much.

This commitment does not mean avoiding areas where we are weak. Growth often requires stretching ourselves. But we must also accept that not everyone is funny, imposing, or charismatic, and there is no need to strive end-

---

PERSONAL NOTES—Erik

My dating history could be described as the exact opposite of authenticity. I exhausted myself in the endless pursuit of the right clothes, the right words, and the right romantic experience to turn ambivalent first-dates into something more. I was always pretending to be someone I wasn't, hoping that love was truly blind and this person would overlook my many faults.

One girl, however, quickly saw through my Oscar-worthy performances. She wanted something more than well-rehearsed lines or romantic settings. She asked deep, probing questions. She took her time before letting me hold her hand. She made me pursue her. It felt incredibly freeing, really, to let go of what I imagined I had to be and rest in being who I really was. My projected image was fading, and yet I loved it, or should I say, I loved her for it. That irresistible taste of authenticity—in her and in myself—was intoxicating.

We are married now. I still open doors and send her notes, not because I am trying to impress her—she figured me out long ago—but because I want to show her who I really am and what she really means to me. "We are all a mess," she reminds me when I try to be something I am not, whether at work or at home, or when I am a bit too hard on someone. It's true. I wish I could have learned that long ago. It just took a dance with authenticity to make me realize it.

lessly to be something we are not. Jesus apparently did not feel compelled to write books, create music, or even be particularly humorous. He operated almost exclusively through thoughtful verbal instruction.

Each of us has been uniquely equipped to give one-of-a-kind gifts, and we have every reason to make the most of what we have to give. In the movie, *Chariots of Fire*, Olympic gold medal sprinter Eric Liddle expresses, "God made me fast. And when I run, I feel his pleasure." We must discover where we are fast, and then run.

4. *The decision to break from expectations, cliché, and pat answers when they distort reality.*

Convention and habit pervade our lives like the air we breathe. We learn by osmosis how to greet an acquaintance, the appropriate distance to keep during conversation, and which subjects are unacceptable in polite company. These tacit rules are generally benign. If left unexamined, however, they can subtly deform truth-telling.

Whenever necessary, Jesus breached these molds. While respectable men avoided interacting with females in public, Jesus routinely engaged women in earnest conversation. Although every other popular teacher included fasting in his students' regimen, Jesus did not, eliciting inquiry as to why. And while upstanding citizens gave wide birth to the morally dubious, Jesus chose to share meals—one of the most intimate expressions of friendship in Jewish culture—with prostitutes and drunkards.

Jesus was not merely shaking his fist at his culture. In fact, the vast majority of the things Jesus said and did affirmed the Jewish heritage into which he had been born. It was simply that Jesus would not allow expectations, habits, or cliché to distort his messages.

Following Jesus in this makes our communication crisper and more genuine and increases its impact. Consider your own response to detours from the expected: a battle-hardened general letting a tear slip down his cheek, a CEO admitting a major planning error, a scientist explaining a concept with simple, homey words. As professor of anthropology Dr. Charles Kraft has observed, when a communicator "acts according to our prediction—the communication impact of whatever that person says or does is very low. If, on the other hand, that person acts or speaks in a way that is unexpected in terms of the stereotype, the communicational impact is much greater."[12]

The decisions required of us will often be less obvious. We must especially work to root out phrases that have lost their freshness—and much of their meaning—due to frequent use. A young missionary in Russia spoke often of a "relationship with God" until an inquisitive young woman asked, "Exactly what is a relationship with God?" The phrase did carry meaning for the young man, but he was struck by how much he stumbled in trying to explain what he meant by the cliché. We all do the same, frequently building our communication upon phrases that we have not bothered to define for ourselves in years.

To avoid this trap, we must relentlessly seek words that really *mean what we say.* Authenticity will be lost if our words and actions are consistently squeezed into the mold of thoughtless custom and tired truisms.

Do you recall what it felt like as a child when, after telling a lie, you had to carry it around for weeks? The weight was as burdensome as Pinocchio's nose. Like a low-grade fever, it hung as a backdrop to everything, souring even the most pleasurable activities. The way out would have been so simple ...

As grown-ups, our reasons for deception have changed. The way out, however, remains much the same. Authenticity offers release—the peaceful, school-is-out-for-the-summer freedom that only honesty can bring.

Most of us spend the bulk of our adult lives engaged in the exhausting activity of trying to get others to accept something that does not exist: the only partially-accurate image of ourselves we want them to think is real. Philosophy professor Dallas Willard asserted, "'[G]rowing up' is largely a matter of learning to hide our spirit behind our face, eyes, and language so that we can evade and manage others to achieve what we want and avoid what we fear."[13]

Sometimes they buy it, sometimes they don't. But the eternal vigilance, the constant guard-keeping, the spin control and image management is as emotionally draining as living in a war zone.

The opposite, Willard observed, is childlike openness and transparency. "The child's face is a constant epiphany because it doesn't yet know how to do this ... Those who have attained considerable spiritual stature are frequently noted for their 'childlikeness.' What this really means is that they do not use their face and body to hide their spiritual reality. In their body they are genuinely present to those around them."

The truth will come out eventually anyway. We can fool people, often for long periods of time, but the real us will always begin to trickle through. As Jesus explained, "From the abundance of the heart, the mouth speaks."

Authenticity cuts us free from the terrible weight of impression-making and image-building. Why not just get it over with—and, as an added benefit, relish the powerful communication that comes with it as well?

Yes, the hazards are real. Our image may be tarnished. People will sometimes turn away, preferring a plastic perfection to the ruggedly real.

But ultimately, our power to influence and connect can find lasting moorings only in the reality of who we are and what we have to offer; nothing more, nothing less. As a close friend urged John Eldridge, "Let people feel the weight of who you are, and let them deal with it."[14] If we are to be truly great communicators, we can take no other road.

In the end, what will be said of the communicator who shuns authenticity—who regurgitates conventional wisdom and parrots clichés, skating safely on the surface of life and emotion, presenting a balanced and just-slightly-less-than-perfect personality, perhaps adding for sake of identity a bit of flair in attire or a "passion" for chocolate, travel, or a sports team?

Very likely, nothing.

The façade such communicators create is lackluster at best, as similar to thousands of others as one tract home to the next. Ironically, even while bearing an almost suspicious resemblance to those around them, they provide nothing that draws others to themselves or creates meaningful connection; nor do they inspire or leave lasting impact. They could hardly be said to exist.

No wonder Ralph Waldo Emerson warned, "Imitation is suicide."[15]

After all, what else besides our own *realness* do we have to offer that is truly unique—distinct, matchless, and thoroughly authentic?

TAKE IT WITH YOU ...

Make a mental list of several shortcomings, insecurities, or hopes you rarely have revealed. Ponder why you have held them tightly, and if there may be benefits in sharing some of them with certain others.

Consider a relationship in which you have recently lacked forthrightness. Are you holding back for their good or your own? If it has only been for your own good, consider sharing what is on your mind—gently.

Don't forget discernment. Real transparency is more than verbal nudity, unrestrained criticism, or novelty for the sake of being noticed. It should not be seen as a "shortcut" to instant intimacy.

Reflect for a moment. Are there ways in which you value image more than truth-telling, or impression more than character? Imagine looking back on your life from the end, considering how you will weigh these matters then.

In what ways are you naturally "fast" in communication, and what talents do you wish you had? Identify at least two talents you should develop, and two you can thankfully accept as they are.

Refuse to settle for cliché. Continually seek new words and phrases to convey familiar ideas in ways that will be fresh and more precise. Instead of saying "cold as ice" try "cold as steel on a January night." Instead of telling a friend, "God is faithful," try expressing what you really mean by a phrase like that. (Do you even know?)

Try to think of a new way to be accessible to someone you desire to influence—perhaps spending time together in an activity you would do anyway.

IN A MEDIA AGE,
we assume that ...
Good stories *decorate* effective communication,
adding a sugar-coating to the facts.

IN EVERY AGE,
the truth is ...
Good stories *deliver* effective communication,
and facts mean virtually nothing
unless they are part of a story.

STORYTELLING:

Once Upon a Time ...

If there is a truly global *lingua franca*—a universal currency welcomed across every country and culture, and every age of history as well—it is not English or French, the dollar or the euro, rare spices, oil, or gold. It is the story.

Soot-covered coal miners burrowed deep into the earth, barefoot shepherd girls guarding sun-drenched hillsides, pasty-faced bureaucrats holed up in dreary cubicles—all take pleasure in a tale well told. As communication professor Walter Fisher expressed, humankind could well be labeled *homo narrans*, the creature that loves narrative. Even amid the blurring speed of modern life and technology, stories of all sorts remain as popular as ever, from *The Lord of the Rings* to the ballads of modern country music.

Jesus, however, did not tell stories merely as a garnish—to make a message more agreeable, inject a touch of amusement, or transition into more weighty matters. Stories stood as the very *centerpiece* of Jesus' communication.

*   *   *   *

In September of 1939, the peace of the waning Polish summer was ripped apart by the grinding machinery and screeching bombs of the Nazi *blitzkrieg*. The fight was over almost before it began. Polish resistance, often waged on foot and horseback with decades-old weaponry, tumbled like spilled toothpicks before the German war machine.

Father Maximilian Kolbe, a kindly-eyed Franciscan monk, was forty-five.[1] Under his respected guidance lived more than seven hundred priests and lay brothers who inhabited the largest friary in the world, Niepokalanow, not far from Warsaw.

As Poland fell under Nazi rule, Father Kolbe urged those under his charge to return to their families or join the Polish Red Cross. He and the remaining brothers would make the friary a haven for refugees, among them 2,000 Jews, whom they housed, fed, and clothed.

A year later, a warning came from the Polish underground: Kolbe's name had made the Gestapo's arrest list. Fearing what might happen to those left behind if he fled, Kolbe chose to remain. It was not long before Kolbe found himself imprisoned at the dreaded concentration camp, Auschwitz.

Exhaustion and starvation stalked every prisoner. Still, Kolbe sought to serve those around him as he always had, sharing his food, praying, and comforting. The camp doctor later recalled of him, "I never saw such a sublime example of the love of God and one's neighbor." Before sleep every night, Kolbe moved from bunk to bunk inquiring, "Is there anything I can do for you?" Only when his service was done would he bless the men, then crumple down upon his comfortless pallet.

On a warm July night, grating alarms and the shouts of soldiers shattered the silence. A prisoner was on the loose—someone from Kolbe's section, Barracks 14. By morning, the prisoner had not been captured, and anger kindled in the guards' normally icy eyes. One had escaped, and now the rest would pay.

After roll call, the prisoners of Barracks 14 were not dismissed to work detail. All day long, they stood rigid, broiling in the summer heat. Some collapsed on their own; others fell beneath blows from the butt of an SS officer's rifle. Remarkably, some remained upright until the other prisoners returned from their day's assignments.

With all the prisoners again in their lines, the commandant was ready to deliver his lesson. "The fugitive has not been found," he shouted. "Ten of you will die for him in the starvation bunker." The starvation bunker represented sheer terror. A bullet, gas, even death by beating would have seemed like mercy. It was not merely starvation, but desiccation—the slowly drying throat, swelling tongue, burning brain, shriveling innards.

One by one, Commandant Fritsch picked the unfortunate souls from the weakest of Barracks 14. "My poor wife, my poor children. What will they do?" wept one man as he was pulled from the line.

"Shoes, off!" ordered the commandant once the ten had been chosen. Terror stricken, they obeyed, piling their wooden clogs in a heap. They would march to their death barefoot.

Just then, another prisoner stepped forward. The commandant reached for his revolver, but merely sneered as a feeble figure came to stand before him. "What does the Polish pig want?"

"I want to die in place of one of the men you have condemned." It was Kolbe, his body emaciated but erect, his voice resolute. A buzz passed among the prisoners.

The commandant paused, thinking, then nodded. "In whose place do you wish to die?"

Kolbe indicated the man who had been weeping. "That one."

That man, Gajowniczek, later recalled, "I could only thank him with my eyes. I was stunned and could hardly grasp what was going on. The immensity of it: I, the condemned, am to live, and someone else willingly and voluntarily offers his life for me—a stranger. Is this some dream?"

A moment later, Kolbe was marching, shoeless, toward the starvation bunker. He and the others were stripped naked before they were shoved down into the windowless basement. Then the door slammed shut.

> **"The universe is made of stories, not of atoms."**
>
> —Muriel Rukeyser, American poet[2]

As the days passed, one by one the men succumbed to the burning dryness. Some tried desperately to survive, licking the dank walls and even sipping from the refuse bucket. It did no good.

But outside, while normally only howls and cries of anguish could be heard, the faint sound of singing drifted up from the pit of suffering. Father Kolbe was leading the men home ...

Ponder for a moment the profound power of such a story.

Could any dictionary better capture the definition of sacrificial love? Could any impassioned instruction or moral plea more inspire a hearer to living—and dying—unselfishly? Could any set of facts and statistics better convey grace amid cruelty, or true life amid death?

*　　　*　　　*　　　*

Matthew, the taxman-turned-disciple, observed that Jesus expressed almost everything he wanted to convey through stories. As already noted, Matthew's sweeping conclusion is remarkable: "He did not say *anything* to them without using a parable."[3]

These parables, as discussed in chapter two, were designed to bring abstract ideas and hard-to-grasp truths into the gritty reality of ordinary life. They were almost always stories. And his listeners—most of them, at least—loved it, paying rapt attention to the tales of lost coins and lost treasure, loving fathers and compassionless clergy, day laborers and homebuilders, wretched beggars and crafty businessmen.

Occasionally, usually with smaller groups, Jesus resorted to more direct, explicit means of conveying ideas. But, always, he would soon return to narrative—weaving stories of seeds and sheep, pearls and pigs, kings and camels.

In the end, noted Bud Paxon, the founder of America's largest broadcast television station group, "He left us one sermon, and dozens of parables."[4]

Of course, Jesus did not have to communicate this way. As screenwriter Dudley Nichols observed, Jesus "could have chosen simply to express Himself in moral precepts; but like a great poet He chose the form of the parable, wonderful short stories that entertained and clothed the moral precept in an eternal form."[5]

Madeline L'Engle, author of *A Wrinkle in Time* and other compelling tales, expressed her conclusion more succinctly in the words of one of her friends: "Jesus was not a theologian, but a God who told stories."[6]

*　　　*　　　*　　　*

Watch those around you the next time you are listening to a speech or sermon. What happens when the speaker ends a sentence that began something like, "It is therefore critical to recognize ..." and launches into, "It was a stormy night in early

PERSONAL NOTES—Jedd

The room was nearly full, most every seat filled by an ardent environmentalist. Only a handful knew me, but all were well aware that the Legislator on whose behalf I would be speaking often crossed swords with groups like theirs. I could see people whispering and gesturing as I walked to the front.

"My father is a high school teacher in the little town of Atwater," I began. "But when I was a boy, each June our family moved to the Sierra Nevada Mountains, where Dad worked as a horse patrol ranger in Yosemite ..."

I recounted how the whole family lived all summer in a little tent cabin. The four boys spent our days rock climbing, fly-fishing, and working in the campgrounds. It wasn't until I was twenty-one that I ventured elsewhere for the summer, to Moscow.

Living in Russia was fascinating, but I ached for California's mountains. So, to survive my first summer away from the Sierra, I pored over John Muir's book, *My First Summer in the Sierra*, imaging the scenes he described and memorizing passages. Even at the office, my screensaver rolled continuously with Muir's words, "Nevermore, however weary, should one faint by the way who gains the blessings of one mountain day. Whatever his fate—long life, short life, stormy or calm—he is rich forever." Muir got me through that summer, I explained, but I'll never pass another without at least one foray into the Sierra.

The story was simple, but heartfelt. And though the audience was aware we might not agree on every issue, they knew I cared deeply about many of the things they valued. Had I tried to convey that fact directly, it likely would have only spawned skepticism. The story, however, opened doors facts alone never could.

winter ..."? Suddenly, faces look up. Doodling pens pause. Even fidgeting kids sit still, at least for a moment. Thoughts of, *When is this going to be over?* instantly become, *What happens next?* The audience actually wants the speaker to go on.

Why? Because people love stories. We love sparking our imagination, our senses, our emotions, visiting new lands, distant frontiers, far off ages. We love loving characters, and despising them. We delight to find a person like us in a story, and to catch familiar glimpses of others we know. We want to find out how things are going to end up, where they will go, what will happen. Stories stir us—heart, mind, and soul.

Simply put, no communication is more enjoyed than stories.

Stories keep people listening too. In at least one remarkable instance, the eager crowds that had ventured to a distant lakeside to hear Jesus remained captivated by his stories for three days straight. Even after their satchels of bread, dried figs, fish, and other victuals ran out, the crowds remained, captured by his simple tales and the profound truth they contained. Jesus had to direct his disciples to find food for them to eat, or the people might well have listened until they were utterly famished.

It is almost as if stories contain a nourishment all their own. A good story "has the same effect on me that I suppose a good square drink of whiskey has on an old toper," stated President Abraham Lincoln, "it puts new life in me."[7]

While merely transferring new information quickly grows wearisome to a listener, well-told stories invigorate—quickening interest, stirring the imagination, and beckoning onward in exploration. Notes writer and management consultant Art Kleiner, "... You can't make someone listen; you can only entice, inspire, cajole, stimulate or fascinate. Stories do that."[8]

In short, no communication causes people to want to listen to what we have to say like stories.

An old Jewish parable describes Truth arriving in a village on a wind-swept night, shivering and bare. At every door, she begs aloud to be let in, but not one is opened. Her nakedness and destitution cause all who see her to wince and turn away. When the old shepherd, Parable, finds her, Truth is huddled alone on the edge of town. Pitying her, Parable takes Truth in, tends her needs, and clothes her in story. So dressed, she returns to the homes in the village. Door after door is opened wide, and Truth, now garbed in story, is received with welcome and joy.

The stories Jesus told accomplished this well, opening doors for the truth he shared, and even drawing people out from their homes to receive his teaching on mountainsides and lakeshores.

Not only bookish students and scholars came. Stories dress concepts and ideas in a form capable of enchanting both large-eyed children and cynical old lawyers; they entertain illiterate laborers as well as sophisticated intelligentsia; they grip the imagination of wiggly boys and distracted young mothers.

In fact, no communication opens the hearts of a more diverse audience.

Jesus himself indicated that he used stories as a way to deliver to each unique listener just what he or she was ready to receive. Jesus welcomed all comers. Still, he knew that while many sincerely longed for truth, some who joined the crowds had little interest in learning; they desired only to be entertained, or perhaps to critique and condemn.

In Jesus' stories, each individual was given what he or she was looking for. The easily pleased novelty-seekers and hardhearted clerics found stimulation, but they often remained "ever hearing, but never understanding ... ever seeing but never perceiving."[9]

The earnest and humble, however, encountered profound wisdom in the simple, accessible form of stories. Each sincere learner, from the simpleton to the sage, was provided with just as much depth and complexity as he or she was willing to receive.

No communication better meets people where they are.

* * * *

The Middle-Eastern monarch slouched, restless in his throne. He seemed to sense the rumors, buzzing like flies over dung in the spring air. It was whispered that the king, despite his reputation for justice and goodness, had taken the wife of a faithful soldier and then ordered the man murdered before he could discover the offense. Whether or not the courtiers believed it, not one would dare breath the accusation in the king's presence.

The throne room fell silent as an old man with a ragged beard hobbled up its steps, the revered prophet Nathan.

Normally welcoming, the king's eyes narrowed, and his jaw tightened. But as the wizened prophet transitioned from his respectful greeting into a simple narrative, relief washed over the room.[10]

"There was peasant who owned a single ewe lamb," began Nathan. "This lamb was a pet to him and his children. It shared his food, drank from his cup, and even slept in his arms. He loved it like a daughter.

"Nearby lived a rich landholder, wealthy beyond measure. He owned vast lands pasturing countless sheep. But when a visitor arrived at his estate, the rich man did the unthinkable. Rather than use a sheep from his own fields, he directed his servants to go and steal the peasant's precious lamb, then prepare it for his guest."

The king rose from his chair, enraged. "How dare that wealthy man do such a thing. He deserves to die!"

The old prophet looked the king squarely in the eye, his voice firm. "*You* are that man."

The air quivered for a moment, tense as a straining bow. Then the king crumpled back into his throne, and let out a long, weary breath. The message had struck its mark.

Every one of us harbors issues we would prefer not to confront. We each hold views and opinions we do not wish to have challenged. As anthropology professor Dr. Charles Kraft explained, "We ordinarily seek at all costs to maintain our present equilibrium, to protect ourselves from assimilating anything that will upset our psychological balance."[11]

As a result, communication that asks us to make anything but the most superficial changes is generally unwelcome to the human psyche. The trouble is, communication often involves just that—requesting change, or expressing truths that can disturb comfortable habits and assumptions.

Stories are uniquely capable of knocking at the door of the

heart softly. They arrive as welcome visitors, neither threatening nor combative. Once invited in and set down by the fireplace, a story can then deliver the truths that need to be heard.

"Advice is like snow;" said Samuel Taylor Coleridge, "the softer it falls the longer it dwells upon, and the deeper it sinks into the mind."[12] In the right context, stories fall softer and sink deeper than any other form of persuasion.

*   *   *   *

Like the prophet Nathan, Anna Leonowens needed to deliver a difficult message to an Eastern autocrat. Serving as a tutor within the palace of King Mongkut, ruler of Siam, Anna desired to help the king grasp how evil slavery really was. She knew, though, that a direct appeal would insult his pride and make change impossible. Mongkut would never govern based on demands from a foreigner, let alone a woman. He must come to the conclusion on his own.

Also like Nathan, Anna resorted to story. She introduced the King to the book *Uncle Tom's Cabin*. Anna hoped that the indubitable humanity of the slave, Tom, and the despicable treatment he received from his master, would draw the king to his own self-discovered condemnation of slavery—just as it had for a great many Americans prior to the Civil War.

The exact details of Anna's efforts and their impact are debated by historians. We know, however, that Mongkut's son reversed centuries of Siamese tradition, allowing his slaves to go free.

The ancient Greeks referred to this approach to persuasion as *enthymeme*—essentially, leaving out part of an argument so listeners can reach the final conclusion on their own.

Stories, particularly when their "point" isn't force-fed, become an invitation to this sort of personal discovery. They allow a listener space to reach conclusions on his or her own. As discussed in chapter three, such self-discovered conclusions ultimately impact more deeply and permanently than those handed to us pre-processed on a silver platter.

Of course, it requires self-restraint to leave it to the audience to notice what we so much want to put right in front of their noses. We must resist fear that they may end up at an entirely different conclusion than we intended.

This danger, however, is inherent to all forms of communication. It is delusion to assume we can somehow "insert" new ideas into another person's brain, whole and unprocessed. In the final analysis, the power of persuasion resides in the mind of the listener, not the speaker. Whatever we wish to convey, it is the listeners who ultimately digest, establish meaning, and decide what role new ideas will have in their lives.

By acknowledging this reality, the communicator using stories actually has a greater hand in guiding the outcome. A mere fact-giver delivers new information, but ultimately remains at the mercy of the receiver's processing. The storyteller provides not only new information, but also offers a compelling framework for how that information can be integrated into the listener's life.

Stories lead, gently and effectively, to the most powerful form of learning: self-discovery.

*   *   *   *

Gary Haugen directed the United Nations' investigation of the genocide in Rwanda. Prior to arriving in the African nation, he had heard almost everything there was to hear about the atrocities that occurred. Personal study, state department reports, and pictures from the evening news filled his mind with details and images. It was not until he encountered Rwanda firsthand, however, that the tragedy became real for him. Looking back, he wrote, "It seemed *true*, but not real—not to me. I did not dispute the accuracy of the reports, but they might as well have been pictures from Sojourner on Mars or reports about people who lived in ancient Rome ... all true enough, but not real."[13]

The simple truth is, our capacity to see the full scope of reality is limited. We can grasp—really *feel* the reality of—only a fraction of those things we have not personally encountered.

Stories are uniquely equipped to help with this dilemma. They can give those who receive them eyes—eyes to see that which would otherwise have remained fuzzy and far off.

This is why the organization Haugen established, the International Justice Mission, builds its communications upon stories. After every completed operation, whether rescuing young girls from forced prostitution or freeing children from slave labor, the events are translated into a compelling story. Without these stories, many Westerners with the capacity to support the work would find it nearly impossible to *see* the suffering or injustice that had cried for remedy, nor would they grasp the joy that comes as justice is restored. Story-given eyes can behold things too terrible—sometimes too wonderful—to believe without seeing.

Storytellers like Eli Wiesel, Alexander Solzhenitsyn, and Rigoberta LePeu-Menchu have been awarded the Nobel Peace Prize for this very reason. Their stories have given an incredulous world eyes to see the depths of human evil—an evil against which we must remain in constant vigil, even within ourselves.

In much the same way, it can be difficult to grip the reality of truths at the other end of the spectrum as well—things that are beautiful, noble, or worthy of our sacrifice.

It frequently takes narratives like those of Abraham Lincoln's many lost elections, Thomas Edison's countless failed experiments, or Albert Einstein's struggles in high school math to enable us to see the value of perseverance and hope.

It takes a story like that of the priest in *Les Miserables*—who rescued Jean Valjean from returning to prison despite Valjean's attempt to steal from him—to enable us to grasp the profound power of mercy.

It takes a tale like Jesus' account of a rebellious son—who took half of all his father owned and pilfered it away on prostitutes and wild living, yet was welcomed home and forgiven all—to make real the lavish forgiveness of an infinite God.

It takes an account like Fredrick Douglass' rise from slavery to becoming a prominent statesman to make believable the promise and possibility our world contains alongside all of its suffering.

This is at least part of the reason Jesus explained the "kingdom of God" not with statements or formulas, but with stories. He knew the things he wished to portray would be novel and beyond his listeners' typical experiences. So he told tales of hidden treasure, gleaming pearls, and an enemy sowing seeds in a farmer's field. Each story gave its hearers an *experience*—partial but poignant—of the reality upon which he urged them to build their lives.

Stories help communicators to turn the *true* into the *real*, whether the darkest edges of human experience or its grandest possibilities.

*   *   *   *

Jesus' consistent focus upon enabling his listeners to sink their fingers into difficult-to-grasp concepts may well have been the most potent element in all of his communication.

Consider some of the most important words in any language—*justice, truth, love, goodness, grace, faith.* As familiar as the terms may be, they are frequently used in ways that leave the concepts they represent vague and distant. The words carry a distinct beauty, like sun-painted clouds, but often remain removed from the dirt and steel of ordinary life.

Communicators allow this to happen in other ways as well. Business consultants toss around terms like "paradigm shift" and "synergy." Pastors describe "living by faith," and political leaders speak of "American values." All too often, the audience ends up with few clues as to what the concept would actually look like if they met it in the street.

Jesus never left an idea or concept floating, abstract, and fuzzy-edged. Never did he refer to vague truths or general principles without immediately connecting them to something in the real world of actions and objects. He rooted every concept firmly in the tangible and concrete.

Note how he did it.

Jesus could have offered a generalized maxim, "Don't focus on the shortcomings of others without first addressing your own." Rather, he painted the jarring word-picture of a man who has a beam poking out of his eye trying to pick a fleck of sawdust from the eye of another. He could have simply stated that putting his instructions into action would be "wise." Instead, he described a man constructing a home upon a foundation of stone.

Jesus never spoke of a far off, spiritualized final reckoning before God. He conveyed images of a shepherd dividing sheep and goats at the end of a day, a farmer picking apart grain from weeds, and a fisherman pulling up a net full of fish and then separating the good ones from the inedible ones.

Jesus could have urged his followers to be a "positive presence" in their community. Instead, he portrayed light spilling out from a lamp throughout an entire house, and the tangy zest of salt, preserving and flavoring food.

Speaking of the world's need for what his disciples had to offer, he did not dryly describe "real opportunities for service," but instead painted the scene as "fields white for the harvest"—an image they would instantly be able to see, feeling with it the rich promise of ripe grain and the urgency of acting quickly to bring it in before the rain.

When possible, Jesus' teaching became even more specific and tangible than stories and word pictures. He often directed attention to objects immediately at hand—a small child he led up before the crowd or an impoverished widow dropping a penny into the temple offering.

Whatever we wish to communicate—trying to explain the word "justice," teaching first graders about the stars, or arguing why a city needs more buses—language that brings our thoughts into the realm of the tangible and concrete will almost always leave the deepest and most lasting impression.

This is what Jesus consistently did. No idea remained distant, abstract, theoretical, or generalized. Whether using stories, metaphors, or physical examples, every concept could be smelled, seen, tasted, heard, or touched.

*   *   *   *

In the disturbing film, *Memento*, viewers enter the experience of a man who knows facts, and nothing more. Severe head trauma has left Leonard Shelby incapable of making new memories. If he is to recall anything, he must create mementos by scratching quick notes on scraps of paper, taking Polaroid photos, and even inscribing messages on his body via tattoo. The recorded details accumulate: He is staying at the Discount Inn; Teddy cannot be trusted; Natalie has lost someone she loves; the person who killed his wife was a white male with access to drugs. Shelby's world overflows with facts. Even so, it is clear that he is utterly lost, for Shelby has no story.

It is sobering to realize how little facts mean without story. Essentially, nothing.

Facts alone convey no more meaning than do strands of thread piled in haphazard tangles on the floor. Stories weave these threads into tapestries, suddenly creating context, value, and significance.

For Jesus, reality itself was woven of story.

The heartbeat of Jewish faith, as Jesus presented it, had little to do with dusty theologies or requirements of legalistic virtue. It was the expansive story of a God whose beloved creatures had rebelled against Him, and of His tender pursuit to draw those wayward children home. Narrative was not merely a means of telling *about* deeper reality; this Narrative *was* deeper reality.

Embroidered throughout this grand epic were countless smaller narrative accounts as well, each revealing unique truths about the character of this God, and His quest to rescue self-willed humankind: a woman's encounter with a devious serpent; a young farmer driven by envy to slay his brother; a flood sent to purge the earth of evil; a slave elevated to Pharaoh's right hand; a stuttering shepherd who became an agent of deliverance; the list could go on for pages.

Of course, this story-based reality spills out far beyond the pages of Jewish Scripture. It is indelibly stamped upon all of human experience. As British journalist Malcolm Muggeridge observed, "History consists of parables whereby God communicates in terms that imagination rather than the mind, faith rather than knowledge, can grasp."[14]

Living in such a universe, the advice offered by storyteller

Annette Simmons merits pondering: "[Your listeners] *have* enough information. They have all the facts and statistics they could ever want. In fact, they are drowning in information. Depression is at epidemic levels because of all this information simply leaves us feeling incompetent and lost. We don't need more information. We need to know what it means. We need a story that explains what it means and makes us feel like we fit in there somewhere."[15]

That is what Jesus' stories did. Our stories can do so as well.

Each of our lives, and all of human existence besides, is a treasure trove of stories. We need not be a globetrotter, statesman, or celebrity. As expressed by Isak Dinesen, who wrote the epic *Out of Africa*, "To be a person is to have a story to tell."

Nor is it necessary to master the skills of a bard. All we need do is sink our hands into the soil at our feet—the delightful surprises, bruised expectations, moments of clarity, and hours of darkness that make up every human life—and then offer them

---

PERSONAL NOTES—Erik

"Uncle E," a voice squeaked from behind me, breaking miles of silence, "can you tell me a story?"

"Ah, sure, Abby," I responded half-heartedly with a quick glance in my rear-view mirror to see her little frame perched on the car seat. My mind flipped through old memories for long-forgotten stories, fables, or nursery rhymes. A story. A children's story. Was that my turnoff?

"There was this horse," I thundered dramatically, as if I was onstage for opening night at the Imperial Theater. An interruption.

"What's her name?" Abby peeped. I flipped on my high-beams.

"Blackie," I proposed. As black as the night.

"Blackie?" she questioned.

I felt the need to press on, despite any clear direction. "Yes, Blackie was a horse, and she was lost," the pace of my story quickening as I turned off the highway. Lost, like us.

"Her name is Yellow Horse," she corrected. "And her best friend is Little Dog. And they work at the circus."

"Why don't you tell me a story, Abby?" I suggested, realizing she wanted me to tell a story she already knew—a story told and re-told by her grandfather hundreds of times.

And so she did. There it is. The right road. The familiar sights. The safe place. Why are stories able to lead us out of darkness and back to familiar places? Why do we long to hear the same story told over and over again?

"And they lived happily ever after," she concluded. "The end."

Our car pulled into the parking spot. We had arrived.

for others to experience as well. Even the most ordinary of happenings, shared with a bit of energy and creativity, can carry significant impact.

Of course, like any art, the skill of storytelling invites a lifetime of exploration, learning, and practice. A handful of simple guidelines are enough to launch the voyage—guidelines sufficiently durable to remain useful even to a practiced storyteller.

• *Succinctness is a virtue.* Avoid rambling by having a clear picture of *why* you are telling a particular story. Hone the story to focus upon that central theme. Eliminate rabbit trails that contribute little to that focus and minimize irrelevant characters, facts, and details.

• *Despite the value of brevity, details and descriptions are critical.* Listeners enjoy stories far more when made to feel as if they are there. A good storyteller, like a cartoonist, needs only a line or two to sketch out a scene, character, or situation. A street "littered with garbage, glass, and broken dreams …"; a face "that protruded like a shark's …"; a beggar "so destitute the dogs licked his sores …"

• *Show, don't tell.* Never say, "It was hot." You want them to *see* hot: "Sweat trickled down my neck, and even the Golden Retriever lay sprawled in front of the fan."

• *Engage all the senses, not just the eyes.* Include smells, sounds, tastes, and touch sensations: the nose-wrinkling odor of formaldehyde; the forlorn cry of a raven; the sharp bitterness of a lemon wedge; the cold rubber of a corpse's skin.

• *Your audience needs to wonder, "What happens next?"* Take a little extra time to build up the unsolved problem, the unexplained mystery, the inescapable dilemma. Suspense—even in very mild forms—keeps people listening.

• *Use every tool at your disposal.* Aid your telling with your hands, arms, and body. Make faces. Use props or reference objects standing nearby. Make sounds and mimic voices. Push your inhibitions a bit.

As with physical exercise, in learning to tell stories well, the most important rule is a simple one: Just do it.

In the end, we must remember our own personal story—lived, not spoken—is the most powerful story of all.

Think back to Maximilian Kolbe. Although his profound devotion to Jesus was undoubtedly shaped and guided by the stories Jesus told, it was ultimately the story Jesus lived that inspired Kolbe to his great and final sacrifice in Auschwitz. Kolbe's own life story, in turn, now deeply impacts us as well.

Through the stories we tell and the story we live, each of us communicates daily with the profound power of narrative. If we tell well, and live well—like Jesus, like Kolbe—we will rarely leave those who hear us unchanged.

TAKE IT WITH YOU ...

Build a reservoir of your favorite stories. When you experience or hear a story that touches you, write it down on a note card, notebook, or in your computer for later use.

Never leave abstract, big-picture concepts floating, disconnected from day-to-day experience and tangible reality. Move quickly from the general to the specific using word pictures, examples, personal experiences, and stories.

Remember that facts mean little outside of stories. Make it a primary goal to weave any new information you wish to convey, and even the information your listeners already have, into stories that hold real meaning for their day-to-day reality.

Pay attention to good storytellers—speakers, writers, screenwriters, or otherwise. Note how they do it. Then, within the realm of your natural strength and comfort level, try to replicate their approach.

Be conscious of opportunities to develop your skills—from describing to a coworker "what happened when my son got sick last night," to scribbling out journal entries before bed. This grows confidence and refines your abilities, especially when you focus upon developing one particular skill at a time.

IN A MEDIA AGE,
we assume that ...
A great communicator makes things happen
from the front of a crowd.

IN EVERY AGE,
the truth is ...
Without time away from the crowd,
we have nothing to offer to it.

CHAPTER SIX

SOLITUDE:
Time Away from the Crowd

Those who consume communication today—and that includes all of us—hunger for more than we are getting.

That is not to say that we cannot be satisfied, often quite easily, by shallow amusements or titillating thrills. Howard Stern and Jerry Springer, among our culture's most-heard communicators, never lack for large audiences. Like the boisterous masses of ancient Rome, we remain sedate and smiling as long as the steady flow of "bread and circus" is not interrupted. As one observer has noted, the whirlwind of confetti amusement "serves to kill time, to lull the faculties, and to banish reflection."[1]

However, just beneath the surface simmers a near desperation for substance.

Instinctually, we long for words that call to us above the cyclone of trivial pursuits, noise, and technologies, wooing us toward something deeper, richer, higher. We ache for a calling deserving of our sacrifice, for pursuits worthy of passion.

In a word, we hunger for vision.

Yet few communicators today can offer such vision. Simply put, we can do no more than *echo* the garbled static around us if we never take time to escape it ourselves. It is a law as incontrovertible as gravity.

Expressing a conclusion reached by many wise women and men throughout history, Mother Teresa of Calcutta observed, "You cannot give what you do not have."[2]

For this reason, Teresa consistently urged volunteers, novices, and fellow Missionaries of Charity at her homes for the sick and dying to spend time in both silent reflection and shared prayer every morning before beginning a day of service.

This time of quietness, of course, could have been employed to lift more sore-covered bodies from Calcutta's gutters and into the Sisters' homes. Countless needs went unmet every day. But although Teresa devoted her life to meeting such needs, she knew that a mere shell of a smiling face could communicate little of the compassion, wisdom, and love the destitute so desperately needed.

That sort of message had to come from somewhere deeper. Only daily time in solitude, prayer, and thoughtful reflection could provide the centering and wholeness that would enable the workers to impart these things to others through the communication of their faces and words.

*   *   *   *

The previous night had been a late one at the home of Simon Peter's mother-in-law in the lakeside town of Capernaum. With the blistering sun finally dipping into the horizon, townspeople began arriving at the door, one-by-one, and in small groups. It was not long before it seemed the entire town had crowded into, or at least around, the modest home. They jostled each other, pressing nearer and nearer to Jesus. All evening they listened, questioned, and strained to hear his voice.

The lamps were guttering, nearly out of oil, when the last visitor exited. A time for long-awaited rest had finally come. Jesus knew the next day—only hours away—would bring more of the same.

Despite the brief sleep, he roused himself early and slipped out the front door, careful not to wake the others. A young woman in the passageway stirred as the door creaked shut. Silence hung over the empty streets. Dawn had not yet broken; stars still reflected from the glassy waters of the Sea of Galilee. Jesus strode briskly to a place where he would not likely be disturbed, perhaps outside of town along the water's edge. He sat alone, thinking, pondering, praying, "My father ..."

As is often the case for great communicators, Jesus' moments in precious solitude would be brief. The eager townspeople were knocking at the mother-in-law's door soon after sunrise.

PERSONAL NOTES—Erik

Wind howled through the Siskiyou Mountains. The pines around me swayed like lumbering giants, retreating from the summer storm that billowed on the horizon. This place terrified me with its aloneness, a forestry station forty-five minutes from the closest town. I was seven years old, and since moving to southwest Oregon from California, this was my first experience with solitude—a place without the sounds of traffic, television, or even a passing airplane. I wanted nothing to do with it.

Maybe time erases old fears. Certainly, life is busier and compressed these days. I long for a place like that now, with natural sounds of wind and rivers that remind me of my smallness. My mind drifts to the trails I never hiked, the trees I was once too afraid to climb.

Solitude and silence arrive infrequently these days, often unannounced—a lunch at my desk, a long drive without the radio, or an early morning walk. To be honest, it's not nearly as much as I need. But I draw strength from these moments, even if brief. The world howls through my life, and I long for the deeper silence that haunted those trees in Oregon—a space uncluttered, without noise. If I am to have it, I must seek it.

Peter and some others set out to find Jesus, apparently oblivious to how much he valued the time alone. When Peter found him, he fixed Jesus with a where-have-you-been stare and exclaimed, "*Everyone* is looking for you!"

Jesus, of course, was well aware his presence and words were in demand. That is precisely why he traded an hour or two of

117

sleep for time alone. For Jesus, solitude and quiet, reflection and prayer, were lifeblood.

This was not an isolated incident. It was the rule. Noted the physician Luke, "Jesus often withdrew to lonely places and prayed."[3]

As Dallas Willard observed, these times of chosen solitude, deprived of noise and activity and friendly interaction, were not enfeebling, dull, or even lonely for Jesus. They were "the primary place of *strength* ..."[4] From these moments flowed the very content and character of Jesus' communication. In those quiet hours, he cultivated the insight and wisdom that could disrobe convention and strip false assumptions naked. Piercing insight. Rock-solid wisdom. Real vision.

No wonder everyone was looking for him.

*   *   *   *

It almost seems that modern life is *designed* to prevent meaningful time alone in quietness, reflection, and prayer.

On some level, it actually is. Providers of goods and services make their profits when you are interacting with their products, not off in quiet reflection. Moviemakers do all they can to get you to watch; restaurateurs urge you to dine; storeowners push you to shop. Your boss could use more hours at work, and the church looks for your attendance and aid. Family and friends, too, want more of your time.

Most of these engagements are legitimate, even desirable. But the net result is that virtually every influence in our lives is working to see that we *do not* spend moments alone in quiet solitude—at least, not if that choice would take time away that we currently give to them.

And we go along with it daily, led like lumbering bulls back into the mad arena. It escapes our notice that the ring in our nose pulling us forward is forged of almost nonsensical assumptions from our culture: busyness equals importance; continuous activity is the key to meaningful existence; you must be going somewhere if you are always moving.

Sometimes we feel exhausted by the constant activity, at others, exhilaratingly buzzed. Often, it is some combination of both. But whether we notice it or not, our pattern of life works its effect on our ability to see with clarity and insight. Almost imperceptibly, it begins to blear and smear. Our capacity for vision grows increasingly blurred.

> **"Prophets, apostles, preachers, martyrs, pioneers of knowledge, inspired artists in every art, ordinary men and the Man-God, all pay tribute to loneliness, to the life of silence, to the night."**
>
> —A.G. Sertillanges, French Dominican scholar[5]

Amid these wearying patterns of activity, even our moments of escape often involve little more than passive consumption of media.

At times, it is hard not to notice a parallel to Aldous Huxley's *Brave New World*, where residents of the future resort continually to the drug *soma* for stimulation, relaxation, and comfort. Our ubiquitous drug of choice is not *soma*, but media. We ingest the substance constantly, from the morning newspaper, pre-work Internet check, and commute-time radio to the lullaby of late night TV just before sleep.

And so, images and sound pervade most every leisure hour. As Italian film director Federico Fellini described, all of this, particularly television, "has mutilated our capacity for solitude. It has violated our most intimate, private, and secret dimension."[6]

Although we might like to think otherwise, this diet will rarely nourish real vision.

The simple truth is that most of the media we consume is

not being supplied to educate, motivate, or even provide rest. Its primary purpose is to keep us watching. After all, advertisers pay for viewers and listeners, not meaningful content. Just like the Ivory-selling soap operas of old, even news programs rise or fall based on their ability to hawk products to a rapt audience. Audiences are less captive today than ever, so they must be captivated; they must be *entertained*.

In some cases, the entertainment takes the form of tawdry daytime talk shows or reality TV. For more "sophisticated" consumers, it is delivered via political talk shows, documentaries, and twenty-four-hour news. The format is a secondary concern. What matters is the ability to sell merchandise— whether soap or cars, fast food, or chewing gum.

The only essential, observes Robert MacNeil of the *MacNeil-Lehrer News Hour*, "is to keep everything brief, not to strain the attention of anyone but instead to provide constant stimulation through variety, novelty, action, and movement."

With rare exceptions, watchers receive only a handful of news bits, sound bites, and salacious stories. So after yet another day of media consumption, we find ourselves neither greatly refreshed nor newly inspired; only entertained.

Ultimately, the communication we deliver will resemble the communication we have consumed. In a tragic cycle, *our* audiences may find themselves neither greatly refreshed nor newly inspired by our words; only entertained.

Of course, there is certainly a legitimate place for entertainment, just as there is for exhausting work and even spurts of dizzying busyness. But if our words are to offer more than *just* these things, if we wish to call to others and stir their deeper parts, we must nourish ourselves with something more.

It is critical we realize that the greatest danger for the communicator is not merely finding ourselves with nothing to say. That is the least of our worries.

Far more disturbing is the prospect that we might continue communicating despite having little worth saying. In such cases, we are no longer driven by a desire to move our listeners toward something better and higher. We are in love with the *words* themselves, the *image* we present, and the personal *impression* we leave behind.

In a book that recounts his own decision to pursue regular times of solitude, writer Henri Nouwen confessed, "[W]ords, my own included, have lost their creative power. Their limitless multiplication has made us lose confidence in words and caused us to think, more often than not, 'They are just words.'"[7]

When this is the case, Nouwen warned, "The word no longer communicates, no longer fosters communion, no longer creates community, therefore no longer gives life."

This is the danger we all face, perhaps skilled communicators most of all.

If we ignore this hazard, and simply slog forward, hoping that our techniques and persona alone will cover for the lack of substance, we may very well wake one day to the same recognition as the professor in Milan Kundera's *The Unbearable Lightness of Being*: "And suddenly he realized that all his life he had done nothing but talk, write, lecture, concoct sentences, search for formulations and amend them, so in the end no words were precise, their meanings were obliterated, their content lost, they turned into trash, chaff, dust, sand ..."[8]

*   *   *   *

Expeditions into solitude can take many forms and serve many purposes, especially for the communicator.

Jesus, as well as those who sought to follow his pattern, valued *daily* moments of solitude ... a single hour, perhaps just ten minutes, on a rooftop, walking a hillside, sitting at the water's edge.

But there were also less frequent periods of *extended* aloneness. At least once, Jesus spent forty days straight, unaccompanied, among the jagged rocks and dusty streambeds of the Judean wilderness. Another powerful communicator, the Apostle Paul, also spent a lengthy period of time alone in the desert—as did Moses, King David, and many others in history's pantheon of great leaders.

Those who have embarked upon extended times alone, however, report back to us that the journey to the outskirts of solitude can be at least as significant today as it was for the greats of the past.

First, this time alone—both in short and longer doses—allows for *refreshment.*

Such experiences offer a deep, soul-rinsing rest not accessible among crowds or supplied by the buzz of entertainment. In these times, we reset our focus and renew our strength for the daunting tasks faced by all communicators.

Jesus sought this renewal not only for himself, but also for his disciples. Observing the constant swirl of noise and crowds, questions and dust, he often urged, "Come with me by yourselves to a quiet place and get some rest."[9] This invitation still stands today.

Second, meaningful time alone provides opportunities for focused *prayer.*

Solitude is not isolation. Far from it. For Jesus, time spent in prayer was nothing less than intimate conversation with the eternal God.

In prayer, our own rough-edged language pours out thankfulness, bleeds our pain and doubts, and begs guidance and strength. We also listen, receiving from God's still, small voice what we likely could not hear amid the roar of ordinary life, as Lord Byron aptly described, "In solitude, where we are least alone."[10]

Third, solitude provides opportunity for *focused thought and learning.*

The wise and great women and men of history wait patiently in the ink of countless books, eager to share observations and truths garnered over lifetimes. Surely many of them have far more to add to our perspective than we can garner in the out-dated-within-the-hour infotainment offered in most of today's headlines and primetime.

During such times of reflection and study, we also experience our richest, most formative interaction with God's revealed truth. His eternal wisdom—what the Bible calls "the *logos* of God"—is declared in the wonder of creation, written upon our hearts, and expressed in the Scripture. This message is often muted by the white noise enveloping both work and leisure. But in calmness and quiet, this living Word begins to penetrate, instruct, and inspire—ultimately allowing our own words to do the same in the lives of others.

Finally, as Henri Nouwen described, "Solitude is the furnace of *transformation.*"[11]

The dizzying pace of our lives is itself a sort of anesthetic. Nonstop doses of activity, interaction, and stimulation serve to numb and blur our senses. We can hardly feel pain, let alone discern what habits and choices might be causing it.

This is what Blaise Pascal had in mind when he expressed, "I have discovered that all the unhappiness of men arises from one single fact, that they are unable to stay quietly in their own room."[12] Solitude strips us of these opiates, forcing us to encounter ourselves and the world as they really are.

In the silence, alone, we can no longer ignore the gnawing ache. As the anesthetic wears off, discomfort may increase, but also clarity. We begin to see things for what they are. The

PERSONAL NOTES—Jedd

Solitude and quiet do not always feel inspiring or even refreshing to me. Taking time alone, there are occasions when I start to feel antsy or bored, or as if I'm waiting for something that never arrives. Contrary to what I sometimes wish for, specific directions for life rarely fall from the sky.

As I do make a practice of time away from the crowd, though, I rarely come away empty.

I recall the summer after my freshman year in college. The previous semester had been rich and full, almost dizzying. It had also been thick with questions and doubts, particularly in my faith. I spent many hours that summer alone in the Sierra Nevada Mountains, sometimes hiking or fly fishing, but just as often reading, writing in my journal, praying, and reflecting on life and creation. I do not regret those hours. Even to this day, I see that summer as a turning point in my life, a time of renewed faith, purpose, and clarity.

The mountains remain my favorite place for time alone, although I find extended solitude in other settings as well, sometimes even at home when alone for a weekend. On a daily basis, too, I seek to quiet myself to pray, listen, read, and reflect.

Often, if I enter solitude with a particular question or issue to resolve, I do not find what I sought. Questions often remain unanswered, and issues unresolved. If willing to wait, though, as my spinning world begins to slow, the undercurrents of vision begin to trickle back into my life. I find a renewed clarity and perspective, a rejuvenation of mind and body, renewed thankfulness, and a sense of nearness to God. And I wonder, *Why did it take me so long to return to this quiet place?*

world's gilded promises and our own self-deception lose their beguiling power. Aspects of our lives that carry little value or purpose—thoughtless patterns of behavior, parroted clichés, and unquestioned assumptions—are laid bare. Once exposed, they can be exchanged for words and choices that bear true vision.

*   *   *   *

In the fourth book of *The Chronicles of Narnia*, the peevish Eustace Clarence Scrubb falls asleep on a mound of hoarded wealth. When he awakes, he finds himself wrapped in sinewy flesh and glistening scales. The boy has turned into a dragon.

Initially, Eustace exults in the dominance dragonhood will give him over the other children. However, it is not long before his new identity ceases to be fun. Loneliness becomes misery. The contempt for others that defines his character is slowly replaced by a sense of the value of friendship, and he even begins to feel affection toward individuals he once scorned.

But his dragon-ness remains, and thick flesh still shrouds the boy deep inside. Instructed by the Great Lion, Aslan, the boy-turned-dragon uses his claws to begin peeling off his own skin. His progress is so limited, however, that he finally accepts Aslan's offer to finish the job, knowing it will be painful. Layer by layer, the lion strips back the skin. His claws sink deep, shredding through the scales and tough outer fibers into softer, more sensitive realms. It burns sharply, tearing deeper and deeper. The smarting sting, however, finally achieves its end. Eustace becomes a boy once more.

Solitude can be uncomfortable, perhaps as much so as the peeling back of a dragon skin, layer by layer. Having become accustomed to a cocoon of activity and noise, even brief moments in silence feel prickly and unnatural. Extended solitude can be downright painful.

We are conditioned to consistently high doses of stimulation—news bits, incoming messages, and background noise. A single day without it, even a half-hour, and we begin to experience withdrawals. *Something* is desperately missing, and—like any addict—we feel compelled to grasp for the substance we crave heedless of consequences. We can hardly stand it!

But we *can* stand it.

And we must. Time away from the crowd is not superfluous. At least, not if we desire the character, and ultimately, the *communication*, that offers more than the colorful monotony found everywhere else. The benefits found in solitude—refreshment and strengthening, focused prayer, insight and wisdom, and soul-deep refining—are the wellspring of truly great communication. They produce the quality that is much sought but rarely found in communicators today: vision.

This process, difficult as it can be at times, enriches not only our communication, but all of life besides. Thomas Merton related, "We do not live more fully merely by doing more, seeing more, tasting more, and experiencing more than we ever have before. On the contrary, some of us need to discover that we will not begin to live more fully until we have the courage to do and see and taste and experience much less than usual."

The results will not be instant. Even after we have stepped from the merry-go-round, the dizziness fades slowly. It may take hours, even days, for our thoughts to stop spinning and allow us to enter fully into the experience of solitude.

Everything in our lives will conspire against it. Urgent projects will appear from nowhere. Invitations and requests will pound at the door. Endless to-do lists will cry for attention. Our appetite for stimulation will growl to be fed.

Yet in the midst of all this, the decision to take time away from the crowd remains ours—as difficult, and as simple, as *choosing* to do so. Today.

No one said powerful communication would come easily.

TAKE IT WITH YOU...

Recognize that you will only be able to echo the static around you if you never take time to escape it.

Understand the costs of pursuing solitude—the time taken away from "more important" activities, the initial awkwardness of being alone and in quiet, and the almost irresistible pull toward getting back to work.

Target low-value activities that can be reduced or removed. Give especially close scrutiny to media consumption—particularly TV, Internet, and video games. Even one commute with the radio off or abstaining from Internet or TV for a weekend can open opportunities for meaningful solitude.

Books such as Dallas Willard's *The Spirit of the Disciplines*, Richard Foster's *A Celebration of Discipline*, or Henri Nouwen's *The Way of the Heart* can help guide in the practice of solitude and other disciplines. But remember, reading does not equal doing. Engage the practice as you are learning.

Pursue time alone daily in a place that allows for quiet solitude. Choose a particular focus for the time as well: study, prayer, rest, or simply reflection.

Also seek less frequent periods of extended solitude, at a cabin in the mountains or camping in the desert. Cut yourself off completely from the things that normally "stimulate" you so you can hear what whispers behind the ever-present noise. If you are serious about this, plan it *now*.

Fight the natural expectation of instantaneous results. Character, wisdom, vision ... they tend to grow like oak trees. Commit yourself to the long haul.

In a Media Age,
we assume that ...
Success is getting what you want.

In Any Age,
the truth is ...
Success is giving what you have.

CHAPTER SEVEN

DEFINING SUCCESS:
Fixed Upon the North Star

They may have lived wildly and drank hard, but sailors who forged the high seas in days of old held one seemingly small detail with utmost sobriety. That one little detail, appearing not much larger than a freckle in the sky, could impact the outcome of a journey even more than the speed of a ship, the spread of its sails, or the skill of the deckhands.

Sailors made sure to know which star was the North Star.

Other heavenly bodies spun continuously across the night sky, never fixed. The North Star was different, shining always as the center point, the standard by which seamen could chart their course, log their location, and measure their progress.

Mistakenly set your instruments by any other point of light, and you very well could end up anywhere ... anywhere, that is, except where you want to go.

*   *   *   *

Della Reese, star of the CBS hit *Touched By An Angel*, stands before the congregation at a church in West Hollywood—*her* church; she has traded in her angel wings for a pastor's pulpit. It is a crowded service at the Understanding Principles of Better Living Church, and Della is preaching prosperity.

"There ain't nothin' up there," she says. "So whatever it is you want, need or desire, or just like to have, you better try to get it now, 'cause this is the only time there is. Yesterday is gone. Tomorrow may be for us and it may not."

Getting what you want while you can—that is one definition of success.

Here's another: The frail woman, her sari held together by a safety pin, seemed out of place in a room of presidents and kings. Among these guests, she was an anomaly—renowned for her work, yet possessing little to show for it. Where others had sedans and servants, she could carry all of her possessions in her worn and weathered hands.

One of the leaders, astonished by the woman's devotion to meeting the needs of the desperately poor, asked her if she didn't become discouraged when she saw so few successes in her work.

Mother Teresa answered, "No, I do not become discouraged. You see, God has not called me to a ministry of success. He has called me to a ministry of mercy."

"*Get it now*" versus a "*ministry of mercy*." Each is a guiding star. Each will lead to very different ends.

*   *   *   *

Leo Tolstoy's story, *The Death of Ivan Ilyitch*, tells of a man who is coming to his end.[1] For some time, Ivan has tried to convince himself he will recover, and that the burning pain within his belly will soon fade like any other minor illness. Only as it becomes inescapably clear that death is near does Ivan face the question he has been ignoring all his life: Has he lived well, sought worthwhile goals? Or, was it possible that he had spent himself on selfish and meaningless pursuits?

Other members of the Russian judiciary had no doubts about him. Ivan climbed the political ranks rapidly. He owned a well decorated home in a popular neighborhood. His wife was fashionable, his child healthy, and Ivan himself generally quite well liked. His fellow judges may have pondered what impact Ivan's departure would have on their own career advancement, but there was no doubt in their minds: Ivan was a success.

But Ivan was not so sure. His body now throbbed with a pain the doctors could do no more than mask for a few hours at a time. He lay upon his couch, reviewing his life's journey. And with an ache even worse than the physical pain, Ivan begins to see, "It is as if all the time I were going down the mountain, while thinking that I was climbing it. So it was. According to public opinion, I was climbing the mountain; and all the time my life was gliding away from under my feet."

For a time, Ivan succeeds in battering back this horrible realization. He reminds himself of his many accomplishments, of his admirers and the status of his position. It is not long, though, before the thought roars back into his mind, "Wrong! All that for which thou hast lived, and thou livest, is falsehood, deception, hiding thee from life and death."

It is only here, at his end, that Ivan has realized the awful truth: He has charted his life by false measures of success.

"And as soon as he expressed this thought," Tolstoy explained, "his exasperation returned, and, together with his exasperation, the physical, tormenting agony; and, with the agony, the consciousness of inevitable death close at hand ..."

Well over a century after it was written, this tale still haunts those who read it. The impact is not merely a result of well-written prose. It is because readers know that the story describes countless men and women in every age—people who realize, only as their end draws near, that the light by which they had set their lives was *not*, after all, the North Star.

> "The true worth of a man is measured by the objects he pursues."
>
> —Marcus Aurelius[2]

Perhaps we have imagined that feelings of uncertainty and dissatisfaction in the midst of what appears to be towering success were strictly a present-day phenomenon. History allows no such illusions.

It was nearly three millennia ago that one of ancient Israel's greatest kings, drawing to his end, recorded final reflections in the book of Ecclesiastes. The monarch life had overflowed with stunning accomplishment, vast knowledge, and toe-curling pleasures. After reviewing all he achieved, however, his conclusion sounds disturbingly similar to that of Ivan Ilyitch: "Yet when I surveyed all that my hands had done and what I had toiled to achieve, everything was meaningless, a chasing after the wind ..."[3]

Centuries later, the Roman emperor Septimus evaluated his own life with much the same words. "I have been everything," he recalled, "and it is *nothing*."

It seems all three of these lives could be summed up quite well in the expression of Britain's Sir Mick Jagger: "I can't get no satisfaction."

Such a sense of failure in the midst of unflagging success seems to stalk communicators especially. One cannot help but wonder why so often it is that powerful communication brings such poor results, or why so many dazzling writers, speakers, actors, or musicians end so miserably.

Ernest Hemingway is heralded as one of the greatest writers in the history of the English language. He received the Pulitzer Prize in fiction and the Nobel Prize in literature, drawing writing material from his own grand exploits as a war correspondent, adventure traveler, and bona fide *Don Juan*. At 61, perhaps with his best writing years still ahead, he killed himself with a shotgun.

Marilyn Monroe became an actress known the world over—a symbol of sexuality and beauty for her generation and beyond. In the midst of her career, she opted for an early exit, downing a month's worth of sleeping pills.

Kurt Cobain was considered by many to be the voice of his generation. His album *Nevermind* sold ten million copies in the United States alone and was heralded in 2002 by *Rolling Stone* as the second greatest record of all time. At 27, he overdosed on tranquilizers in an apparent suicide attempt. A few months later, in a cottage overlooking Lake Washington, he

---

PERSONAL NOTES—Erik

"I have cancer," said the familiar voice, breathless and heavy. My stomach dropped like a stone in deep water, leaving my mind swirling with "what-ifs."

"My mom has breast cancer," I told my wife, summing up the entire phone call with a single line—a line that began a difficult year of surgeries, radiation, and chemotherapy sessions designed to bring her body to the brink of death. Mom's bright blue eyes yellowed, and her skin faded to the color of ash. Her curly golden hair was replaced by a bristly, itchy wig. And her mouth, always ready to give kisses to grandkids, was covered by a surgical mask.

On the final day of her treatments, shortly after the doctor declared that recovery had begun, the phone rang again. This time, it was my father's voice: "I have cancer."

Words failed me. I listened without emotion—my tears and anger had been used up in dealing with my mother's sickness. "God, what are you doing!?" I shouted inside. This cancer was far more serious and invasive, casting us back into the now-familiar routine of surgeries, doctor visits, MRIs, and radiation.

Cancer is hardest on the people around the victim, it seems, and I could see it in my mother's face—watching her husband's sufferings hurt more than her own. For both of them, what defined success drastically changed. Success, often gauged via bank statements or number of years until retirement, was now measured in weight gain, doctor's reports, and the return of hair. In one of the many emails my father sent to family and friends chronicling his struggle, he wrote: "The yard stick of success that the world uses is so deceptive and inadequate ... I look back at the wasted years of a life that's on the shadowy side of the hill ... and am struggling to break the momentum of a life [that is] habitually self-preserving."

It's been eighteen months since that phone call. Both Mom and Dad are well—healed from cancer. What remains are the scars and semi-annual doctor's appointments that remind of what they endured ... as well as a deepened sense of what really matters, of true success.

aimed a shotgun at himself and pulled the trigger.

Admiring glances from people around you ... a reputation for eloquence ... articles written and books published ... the power of sexual appeal ... promotions and raises ... invitations to the right homes, the right parties. No doubt, communication fixed in pursuit of such successes gratifies for a time. But if serving as the North Star—the ultimate end and goal—they will not lead true.

The suicide note Cobain left behind may have rambled, but it did not fail to depict the place to which his success had led. No doubt, it spoke for many other renowned-yet-failed communicators as well. "I haven't felt the excitement of listening to as well as creating music along with reading and writing for too many years ..." he wrote.[4] "I've tried everything within my power to appreciate it, and I do. God, believe me I do, but it's not enough ..."

Most of us will never reach the heights achieved by fabled figures like Hemmingway, Monroe, or Cobain. Their endings merely provide us clues, hinting that even the smaller successes we seek may not, after all, bring the satisfaction we often imagine.

In time, most everyone comes face to face with this reality. A man in a California firm watched as a fifteen-year company veteran was given a termination notice and asked to clear out his desk. Bewildered, the fellow placed his personal effects in a box and said goodbye to colleagues he considered friends. By afternoon, his desk was filled by a newly hired manager, who picked up where its prior resident had left off. *If what defines my life is measured in sales records, pay increases, or promotions*, realized the man who had observed the seamless replacement, *I'm lost.*

*   *   *   *

"Executive enhancement" is how the highly sought-after image consultant describes her work. Her company takes frustrated job-seekers, failing executives, overlooked assistants, and socially-impaired salespersons and teaches them to "psych out others and ... get what you want."[5]

In her popular book, the consultant promises that "success comes to people who are *versatile*, who can make a smashing *impression* in any setting, who can identify their peers' or managers' *hidden agendas*, and use *psychodynamics*—the science of human behavior—to get what you want."

Guided by such a perspective, the power of psychodynamics becomes more important than either character or providence. "In the real world," the author concluded, "it's the combination of connections, charm, and finesse that makes the cream rise." In this "real" world, success is a science—a mastery of techniques and tactics, a manipulation of people and professions, and a winner-take-all, take-no-prisoners ambition.

As we are well aware, this is just one of countless formulas for success hawked by best selling books, well-dressed consultants, and pricey self-help CD series. Each offers its own unique definition of success. Indeed, the night sky is full with would-be North Stars, every one glittering with a golden promise to guide us to the purpose and happiness we long for. It can be painfully difficult to discern which will lead us true.

The dilemma is particularly pressing in the realm of communication. Should we measure success by applause? The size of our crowd? Whether or not we can bend others' will to align with our own, or make them like us? Our ability to rouse physical attraction, or elicit admiration in the eyes of another?

For most, communication success boils down to the *reaction* of the audience—be it a lover, a friend, a small group, or a full auditorium. A laugh means we are funny. A standing ovation means we are accepted. A nod means we are connecting.

Receiving the desired response, we are taught, is the standard of success.

But such a standard is stunted at best. As Thomas Merton observed, "The logic of worldly success rests on a fallacy: the strange error that our perfection depends on the thoughts and opinions and applause of other men! A weird life it is, indeed, to be living always in somebody else's imagination, as if that were the only place in which one could at last become real!"[6]

Ironically, this audience-obsessed definition of success does not make our communication more audience-centered. It is all about us, the communicator. What do they think of *me*? How am *I* doing? Will *I* be admired, praised, thanked, remembered ... and ultimately get what *I* want?

When this sort of success becomes the North Star, other people are reduced to means. They become objects to be moved and molded in ways that help us achieve our self-interested ambitions: admiration, clout, connections, financial gain, false forms of intimacy, or professional advancement.

With our eyes fixed solely upon these ends, our communication becomes little more than manipulation. Without even being aware of it, we begin to seek words and techniques that yield automatic, push-button responses. The desired results, we hope, will follow like a candy bar dropping from a vending machine after the correct change has been inserted, or like a rabbit popping from a hat with just the right wave of a wand.

Jesus' approach could not have been more different.

*   *   *   *

History does not record the dialogue, but it isn't hard to guess. Jesus' disciples were bickering, again, jousting with words over which of them had made the biggest strides, merited the most respect, deserved the right to lead. The voices fired back and forth, hushed but tense.

"You think you're better than the rest of us? Peter and I were the first to join him ..."

"If there are any top lieutenants around here, it's John and me ..."

"It isn't that I'm better, just ..."

"First to join doesn't count for much. What a guy gave up to be here carries a lot more weight ..."

"I left behind one of the most lucrative enterprises in Jerusalem ..."

The twelve disciples had been together for three straight years, almost every waking hour spent side-by-side. Understandably, they had their squabbles from time to time. But this was inexcusable. Tonight was the Passover celebration, a time for celebration and hallowed remembrance. And now, just as the evening was getting started, an argument erupts over rank and relative importance.

"So now you're looking down at fishermen? Didn't you hear what Jesus said to me the other day about ..."

The voices trailed off as the men noticed Jesus' eyes upon them. Silence filled the room, and twelve sets of eyes turned toward their sandals.

Jesus smiled sadly. The lesson had been delivered many times already. Repeatedly, he had instructed his disciples to abandon self-promotion and prideful ambition. He would exhort them one last time: "This is how people *out there* approach success," he reminded. "For them, it's all about position, status, power, and titles. That's not how it's supposed to be with you. Success is in the opposite direction—serving, waiting tables, meeting each others' needs."

As always, Jesus desired to make his words more concrete. He removed his robe and laid it nearby. There was one job that even most house servants considered themselves above—washing the dust and grime from the sandal-clad feet of travelers. The task was reserved for the last-placed servant, the lowest on the totem pole. Wrapping a towel around his waist the way a common slave would do, he took a basin from the sink in the corner. Then, directing his students to sit, Jesus knelt and began scrubbing dirt from their feet.

When he had finished, Jesus rose. As he often did, the teacher led with a question: "Do you understand what I have done for you?" He paused, letting them ponder for a moment. "You call me 'Teacher' and 'Lord,' and rightly so, for that is what I am. Now that I, your Lord and Teacher, have washed your feet, you also should wash one another's feet."

He finished with a simple conclusion: If you pursue this sort of serving, you'll know true blessing.

*   *   *   *

Consider for a moment, to which of the people in your life are you most likely to listen? Whose words do you allow to carry the deepest influence?

If you were to make a list, the majority of these individuals would likely be unified by one outstanding factor: They would be people who care a great deal about you. The teacher who consistently goes beyond the call of duty. The friend who comes by in times of special need. The mentor who aches to see you grow and learn. Their words, even if less than articulate, tend to sink deep and last long.

The ancient Greek masters of oratory understood this principle well. As Aristotle described in *The Rhetoric*, the most influential aspect of a person's communication is their *ethos*—

their character and person. Despite the importance of well-crafted arguments and emotional appeals, *ethos* carries the most gravity.

Clarifying further, Aristotle divided ethos into three elements—"competence," "integrity," and "goodwill." Of the three, goodwill stood central. When listeners perceive that the communicator is sincerely committed to their good, explained Aristotle, it tends to carry more weight than any other factor.

We know this intuitively. Few things make us less likely to listen than sensing that a speaker cares little about us and our concerns. No matter how skillfully expressed, we discount what they have to say and feel little desire to grow close to them.

In contrast, when we perceive a person is committed to our good, we give them fuller access to our hearts. We allow them—and even invite them—to help guide our opinions, shape our plans, and grow deeper in friendship.

With few exceptions, the people whose communication carries the most weight in our lives are those who have defined *their* success as *our* success.

*   *   *   *

Even perched on a small stack of books, Salomon and Mery Hernandez would not reach most Americans' shoulders. Gray now streaks once ebony hair, and wrinkles etch their faces. Their eyes, however, still cast sparks, dark and intense, and ready smiles offer unconditional welcome.

Salomon and Mery are *Ladinos*. Of the two distinct groups in Guatemalan society, the *Ladinos* are the majority—lighter skinned, Spanish-speaking, and generally more Western and well-to-do. On the other side of a vast social chasm are the indigenous Guatemalans, the Mayans. These sharp featured, dark skinned people are set apart not only by their culture and native language, but also by the poverty that dogs their existence.

Decades ago, when Salomon was working as a pastor, the gaping divide between *Ladinos* and Mayans began to gnaw at the young couple. Here they were, seeking to lead people to be disciples of Jesus, yet while the master they claimed to follow consistently slashed against such social barriers, their own church eagerly embraced them.

Together, the young couple decided that Salomon would try to learn *Quiche*, a Mayan dialect others referred to with derision as "the language of the poor." In fits and starts, his vocabulary grew. News began to spread among local Mayans of "the pastor who speaks *Quiche*." First one Mayan, then others, appeared at the church. Some understood little Spanish, grasping only bits of Salomon's messages. Still, the fact that he knew *Quiche* drew them. "This man must care about us," they whispered to each other, "he has learned our language."

The *Ladinos* in the church were not nearly so impressed. Salomon and Mery could not help but notice the concerned glances cast at the newcomers. As time went on, the glances became glares of irritation and muttered complaints. Finally, a group broached the subject with Salomon directly. They explained, "We're not sure it is best to have Mayans in our church. They have many diseases. It is not safe for our children. And their smell ..."

Salomon gently pointed out whom they were supposed to be following. "Jesus continually served people Jews hated, the Samaritans," he reminded. "And lepers, and tax collectors, even prostitutes."

It was not long before the group was back, this time larger. "We have decided we must build a second church building," an elder announced, "One for the Mayans, one for us."

Again, Salomon resisted. "If we are going to follow Jesus, we need to grow *together*. We must learn to love and serve each other as a community," he urged.

Not many were convinced. The ultimatum came a short time later. "Salomon, we will let you make a choice," they offered, eyes cold. "You can either be our pastor, or you can serve the Mayans. Not both. The decision is up to you."

Painful as it was, the path was clear. Salomon and Mery had chosen their course long before. Success was found in serving, and if they were to fail in that regard, little else mattered. Salomon would be their pastor no more.

Since that time, Salomon and Mery have spent much of their lives working with the Mayan people. Some *Ladinos* still think they are fools to stoop so low. But many Mayans claim they have had no better friends than Salomon and Mery Hernandez. And the giving has not been entirely one-sided. Mayan friends delight to invite Salomon and Mery into their homes and to their festivals, or to bring them corn from their fields or freshly-harvested *melanga* root. And more than once during Guatemala's bloody civil war, the couple was rescued from death at the hands of Mayan guerillas by friends they had served.

The Hernandezes will likely never receive a Nobel Prize or international recognition. Even most Guatemalans have never heard of them. But those who have spent time with them know Salomon and Mery have tasted real success. Their daily existence glows with deep and substantive relationships, lasting impact upon others' lives, and a legacy of true service to the people around them.

Admittedly, our cravings and ambitions often pull us in the opposite direction. In addition, the buzzing world of commerce and celebrity rewards anything but this definition of success.

But still, our souls are stirred when we encounter it. Our hearts swell, if only for a moment, with desire to pursue such a path. Imagination, hope, and longing quicken. Emotions that have slept since childhood awake—we want to quest and serve and live for a vision larger than our own petty wants. Deep down, we know Jesus was right, and that the star to which he pointed is indeed the North Star.

Our hearts confirm this truth when we encounter people like Salomon and Mery. Or experience a movie like *Braveheart, Stand and Deliver,* or *Mr. Holland's Opus.* Or recall Clara Barton wading onto a Civil War battlefield or Mother Teresa kneeling beside a child in Calcutta's gutters. Or hear again of the Good Samaritan on the road to Jericho. Or read about Father Damien, the leper priest of Hawaii, or Maximilian Kolbe in the concentration camp at Auschwitz.

The moments of clarity may be brief and our own desires conflicted. But wedged in our hearts, alongside baser motives and selfish ambitions, remains a deeper sense that real life is found only in giving one's self away, in serving. Despite the rugged road along which it leads, something still whispers that Jesus' definition of success will lead us true.

*   *   *   *

So what does it look like to communicate guided by such a North Star—not in momentary bursts of feel-good emotion or holiday goodwill, but consistently and continually?

If we are honest with ourselves, our sense of what servanthood entails is often less than inspiring. We envision a sickly-sweet Betty Crocker smile, or perhaps a spineless Igor answering orders to fetch and carry. If we adopt Jesus' definition of success, we worry that we will become timid, servile, and even degraded.

Those individuals who experienced life with Jesus saw these fears shattered.

Jesus' definition of servanthood was much closer to that of the Japanese Samurai, whose noble title literally meant "servant." These servants were anything but servile or degraded. They were warriors, bold and fearless, as self-disciplined as steel, carrying out with utmost vigor their stated purpose—to honor those in whose service they stood.

Legendary football coach Vince Lombardi, a warrior in his own right, expressed much the same understanding of strength-in-servanthood. This road to true success, Lombardi explained, "... is in sacrifice, it is in self-denial, it is in love and loyalty, it is in fearlessness, it is in humility, and it is in the perfectly disciplined will."[7] The decision between this definition of success and setting our course by other stars, concluded Lombardi, "is the distinction between great and little men."

This is the kind of servanthood that blazed as Jesus' North Star, setting his course in each communication act and in all of life besides: robust, loving, bold, loyal, sacrificial, outwardly-focused, self-denying, disciplined, and continually giving. Despite the crowds waiting on his words and his status as a master teacher, Jesus "did not come to be served, but to serve."[8]

By Jesus' definition, successful communication is *attending to the needs of others through our communication.*

Fixed upon this course, Jesus' every interaction glowed with extraordinary qualities. These traits glimmer in the lives of all servant communicators. If absent, we would do well to consider if perhaps some other star might be setting our course.

Jesus showed remarkable flexibility. Since self-focused ambitions did not drive Jesus, he never appeared obsessed with his own timing or agenda. Inconveniences and changes in plans were not catastrophes. Interruptions—a centurion arriving unannounced or an invalid lowered through the ceiling in the midst of his teaching—became opportunities for success in serving.

Jesus was willing to take great risk. With his focus set on the needs of others, Jesus worried little about how he was being perceived. This left him free from the consuming need to manage impressions that many of us feel. As a result, he could speak boldly and with transparency. He could be seen with outcasts and venture into places where he might be rejected—meeting others where they most needed to be met.

Jesus emphasized the personal. Jesus did not equate larger scale communication with larger good. Time and again he slipped away, just as the crowd swelled, seeking an intimate moment with only a few by his side—in a garden, a boat, or a home. Never did Jesus forsake the one for the many, and often he turned his back on the crowd to focus upon a single long-forsaken soul.

Jesus was remarkably non-coercive. Although his words held great power, Jesus never used them to short-circuit his listeners' decision-making process. He recognized that most of the good he desired to do for others required their willingness to receive. So he resisted the temptation to force-feed medicine or push for the hard sell. Instead, he used questions, stories, and other tools that placed responsibility for discovery and response fully in his listeners' hands.

Jesus favored conciseness. Jesus never said everything that *could* be said in each situation, only what was most needed. Volume of ideas shared did not matter, just what listeners would take with them when they left. His approach was reflected in President Lincoln's 272-word Gettysburg address, not the two-hour speech delivered on the same occasion that history forgot. Jesus quested for a potent brevity because he knew it would carry the most lasting impact.

Jesus remained patient and perseverant. Since the long-term good of others was the goal, real-time results mattered little. Jesus faced continual setbacks and disappointments. His disciples chronically misconstrued and misunderstood, and seemed to forget even the simplest lessons. Yet, because his focus was set on their good for the long run, the letdowns never were more than one small piece of a much larger panorama.

Jesus delighted in the small and insignificant. Jesus did not exult when his reputation blossomed or palm branch-waving fans lined the road. Yet he rejoiced at events others would hardly notice: faith expressed in an unexpected place, a sincere question, or a hint that his disciples had understood a lesson. While Jesus viewed popular success as an enticing illusion, the little victories in individual lives brought him deep joy.

*   *   *   *

The best Olympic athletes set themselves fiercely toward a single goal: the gold medal. This palm-sized disc is the highest symbol of excellence, the zenith of athletic achievement. For the Olympian, gold embodies ultimate success. The athlete's only hope of attaining it is to take on an almost sadistic pattern of life: regimented schedules, bizarre diets, endless hours of training, and indefinite deferral of all other interests.

If viewed through a different standard of success—say, as measured by accumulation of wealth, professional degrees, or mere pleasure-seeking—these choices would make little sense. In fact, they would appear insane. But, if success is a gold medal, everything suddenly fits. The choices and behavior do not just make sense; they are necessary.

Whatever the realm of life, it is the end goal that determines which choices "make sense" and which are foolhardy or worse.

Although some may argue otherwise, it is hard to avoid

PERSONAL NOTES—Jedd

They couldn't have been more than fifteen years old, parentless boys living at an orphanage outside of Moscow. My traveling companions and I spoke to a large assembly that morning, and afterward several boys challenged us to a soccer match out on the snow-crusted field.

Icy patches, heavy jackets, and all, it was a rousing game. Toward the end, though, I began to push my teammates. I didn't want just to play; I wanted to win. I goaded them on, and even got a bit rough in my play with the other team.

That evening, one of my friends called me on it. "What we were there for?" he asked, "It seemed like you were more fixed on winning a game than on connecting with the kids or caring for them." He was right. Even to myself, I would have affirmed a clear purpose for visiting the orphanage: to show love to the children there. But caught up in the game, my actions were guided by an entirely different goal.

In retrospect, it seems silly. The truth is, though, I do it more often that I'd like to admit, not so much in sports now, but in regards to career, financial resources, or reputation. I articulate one definition of success to myself—Jesus' definition—but get caught up in the game. My communication becomes a means not to serve others, but to grow my own position, reputation, income, or status.

If I am to set my communication toward Jesus' North Star, I must consistently take time to question myself and refocus. I also need to be accountable to others who desire to pursue a similar path. Otherwise, it's too easy to get caught up in the game.

the simple truth: If we adopt any standard of success but that of Jesus, his communication practices ultimately fall into the latter category—foolhardy or worse.

Admittedly, Jesus' principles offer great power, even if used merely as tools of influence or techniques for manipulation. Even so, if we are seeking only our own good, the risk and effort Jesus' approach requires will quickly prove too high.

Yes, we may still show attentiveness ... until it requires that we abandon prior plans. We may seek others on their turf and in their terms ... up to the point that it entails risk to our image or our safety. At times we will offer ourselves with transparency ... but usually just enough to give the *appearance* of openness. We will tell stories and ask questions ... until they oblige us to allow others to decide for themselves. We might even take time in solitude ... but merely as a method of self-betterment, not to equip ourselves to serve.

In the end, only Jesus' definition of success will free us to fully live out his communication.

Because he did not measure success in terms of his image, agenda, or self-indulgence, Jesus could give himself fully, risking all, to the very best communication. This path is open to us as well. Communicators who define success as Jesus did will gain the success they seek: They *will* serve through their communication. And, almost unexpectedly, they will discover also the added benefits of impact, connection, and influence—qualities that so many others seek but rarely find.

Does this seem strange? Grasping after these qualities often leaves us empty handed, while questing off in the opposite direction—seeking only to serve—delivers all three.

Ironic, yes. But the world we inhabit is indeed governed by such rules. Run after a cat, and you will rarely catch it; sit quietly, and it will soon be purring at your side. Obsess with guarding your health, and you will always find an ache or pain to bemoan; risk, run, and play with abandon, and you'll almost certainly hike with your grandchildren someday.

As Jesus made clear: Seek to gain your life, and ultimately you'll lose it ... lose your life, and in the end it will be yours.

*   *   *   *

The rolling waves are calling once again. Our vessel will soon be leaving port. Books provide much-needed time within the harbor, but ships are made for the high seas. And whether we like it or not, the course we take will be set by the light we choose as our North Star.

If our benchmark for success rests primarily in attaining self-interested ambitions and pleasure, we will no doubt find at least some of what we seek. There will be moments of savory pleasure and notable achievement. But, in setting such a course, we must also know that we will never be truly satisfied. In the end, the last words we hear may be those of Ecclesiastes:

"Meaningless, meaningless ... a chasing after the wind ..."

Or, we can dare to pursue the course Jesus took, wrought with struggle and storm. Such a decision rejects the known routes. It is subversive, cutting with almost every communication choice against the direction modern assumptions point to as most sensible and gratifying. This is a journey heavy with risk and the unknown.

But amid this risk and sacrifice, there also awaits life's richest rewards: deep connectedness, real communion, lasting companionship. As others are captured by our vision, they will draw near. As they hear in our voices sincerity and authenticity and compassion, they will listen. As they see that our definition of success is *their* success, they will follow.

For those who desire *this* kind of communication, there can be only one North Star.

TAKE IT WITH YOU ...

Take a moment to consider: What do you desire your North Star to be? Ponder carefully. Consider writing your answers down. This decision will set your course and shape the character of your communication more than any other factor.

Regardless of what you want your North Star to be, which star are you following? Do not settle here for the simple answer you would give to others. Look specifically the standards you use to measure your progress and achievement.

As important as all this is, don't overanalyze yourself. Even when desiring to make meeting the needs of others your standard for success, know that your motives will always be mixed. That is okay. Such is life in this world. The best we can do is work to set our hearts in the right direction; we'll never fully arrive on this side of heaven.

> "I have
> nothing
> to offer
> but blood,
> toil,
> tears,
> and sweat."
>
> —Sir Winston Churchill[1]

CONCLUSION

SO WHAT DO I GET?

The Journey, from Trial to Triumph

The history of World War II is a trove of heroic tales. Many of them conclude, however, with no happy ending.

Claus von Stauffenberg was born of military German roots—generals, marshals, and knights filled his family tree. From his first days with the 17th Bamberg Cavalry Regiment, he distinguished himself among superiors and subordinates alike.[2] Even into the early years of World War II, as Stauffenberg grew increasingly disaffected with National Socialist ideology, his record of service on the Eastern and African fronts drew only praise.

In 1943, however, while recovering from wounds received in Africa, Stauffenberg decided he had seen enough of Nazism to know he wanted no part in it. Joining the German resistance, the thirty-seven-year-old officer quickly assembled an impressive network of influential figures around a bold plan. They would strike at the head of the Nazi machine, Hitler himself, and Stauffenberg would deliver the blow.

Stauffenberg and other conspirators readied an expansive strategy for what would transpire after Hitler's death. A wide web of resistance leaders prepared to step into key government and army posts immediately. They stood ready to wrest Germany from the Nazis in a single day.

After two aborted attempts, the awaited opportunity arrived. On July 20, 1944, Stauffenberg would be part of a briefing at the fabled Wolf's Lair; Hitler would most certainly be present. "I have examined myself before God and my conscience," stated Stauffenberg. "It must be done because this man is evil personified."

Stauffenberg gently set his briefcase, with its contents ticking, beneath a map table in the briefing room. Heart racing, he slid from the building. Minutes later, the room exploded. Flames burst from the windows with enough heat to warm Stauffenberg's face fifty meters away. "The beast is dead," he muttered, then stepped into a waiting car, ready to move into the next stage of the insurgency. A new dawn was breaking over Germany.

Hitler, however, was not dead. The heavy oak of the map table shielded him from the brunt of the blast. The beast was injured, but would live.

After the conspirators' initial sense of triumph, news of Hitler's survival fell like an anvil. Attempts to seize power in Berlin quickly floundered. Within hours, Stauffenberg stood before a firing squad, just a short distance from the military office where he had spent months hammering out his plan.

It had all been a dismal failure. Already, Stauffenberg's co-conspirators were being hunted down and killed. Officers he had counted on to join the revolt were reaffirming their allegiance to the Fuehrer. The coup had hardly made a dent. With little trouble, the Nazi machine was again in full control. If anything, the attempt only strengthened Hitler's grip on power. The guns fired, and Stauffenberg fell dead.

Perhaps such tales are not so frequently told. But many accounts of noble characters end thus: heroism crushed by brute force. Great sacrifice that produces only a pittance of hoped-for results. Sweat, blood, and tears sliding off down the drain, leaving but a murky residue in their wake.

Jesus' approach to communication comes with no guarantees. Disappointing ends may await us as well.

Communicating the way Jesus did demands far more than the tricks and techniques that thrive on image and impression. Make-up, lights, and plastic surgery are the easy way. Jesus' route requires practiced disciplines, self-denial, and continual growth.

Even after all the sacrifice and effort, no doubt there will be times when attempts to meet a person in their space meet rejection. Offering ourselves in vulnerability, we may encounter only ridicule or disinterest. Thoughtful questions will receive thoughtless answers, and meaningful stories will be misunderstood. We will listen, but not be listened to; serve, but not be served. Almost certainly, after we have poured ourselves out again and again, we will see only a fraction of the results for which we have hoped.

Such was the experience of Jesus.

Admittedly, his days burned with purpose and relationships and impacted lives. Multitudes waited on his words. Men clamored to be near him. Mothers brought children for his blessing, and former prostitutes washed his feet with their hair. He healed aching hearts and gave lost souls new direction.

But we cannot ignore that virtually every page of the Gospels carries a letdown, a disappointment, an unsatisfactory response to selfless love. Jealous leaders continually sought to interfere and impede. Close companions misunderstood his mission. Relatives remained skeptical, and once-eager followers packed up and headed home. Even loyal disciples continually doubted, bickered, and failed to recall crucial lessons. In the end, Peter, James, and John drifted off to sleep while Jesus sweat drops of blood close by. When his enemies came for him, his best friends turned tail and ran. Crowds he had fed chanted, "Crucify him!" And the leaders of his nation handed him over to occupying foreigners to be killed.

If *that* is the fruit of Jesus' approach to communication, we are sorely tempted to search for smoother roads. Tricks and techniques. Tools of charm and manipulation. Books about psychodynamics or even the Understanding Principles of Better Living Church in Hollywood. Please, anything but Jesus' path.

However, there is more to the story.

Jesus' approach requires the long view. It necessitates eyes so fixed on the North Star that although failure, disappointment, and distress wash all around, the ship will not turn from its course. For indeed, in the long view, we do see in Jesus' life everything that we could have hoped for after all: immeasurable effect upon human souls ... devoted friends who would ultimately give their lives for him ... and shockwaves sent through history itself.

In two millennia, Jesus' legacy is unsurpassed. Many have said what Ronald Reagan expressed on a Christmastime radio address, "... [T]his uneducated, propertyless young man who preached on street corners for only three years who left no written word has for 2,000 years had a greater effect on the entire world than all the rulers, kings and emperors, scientists and philosophers who ever lived—all put together."[3]

That is the fruit of Jesus' approach to communication.

Of course, it would be exceedingly foolish to claim this all was a product of Jesus' communication alone. Indisputably, the profound impact of his life had far more to do with who he was.

This is a matter every honest thinker must ultimately confront: Who was Jesus really? As C.S. Lewis pointed out, the brazen claims Jesus made about himself severely reduce our options. A man who maintains that he is the very Son of God can only be a vicious liar or a raving lunatic—unless he is the very thing he claimed to be. Such bold assertions allow no room to conclude that Jesus was merely a good teacher or, for that matter, merely a great communicator.

Neither can we ignore Jesus' death. The men and women who knew him best claimed Jesus went to the cross not merely in a symbolic gesture or as a condemned revolutionary. Rather, he died a criminal's death and rose from the grave, they argued, to bridge the gap between God and humanity. Some dispute the claims as legend or lies. Yet, those very followers of Jesus were willing to go to their deaths in defense of what they had seen with their own eyes.

Every one of us must engage these vital questions.

In doing so, however, we need not lose sight of the fact that Jesus was a profoundly effective communicator, perhaps the very best the world has ever known. And living these communication truths, he set echoes sounding in human hearts and minds—echoes that have not ceased to reverberate for a hundred generations.

It would seem strange, even nonsensical—especially for those who claim Jesus as the center point of their lives—to fail to become his apprentices in a realm that carries such deep impact upon virtually every aspect of our daily experience.

If we follow Jesus' path, coming to embrace both his practices *and* his person just as his first students did, we can expect similar outcomes: frustrated efforts and moments of deep disappointment, yet at the same time, a fullness of life and interaction beyond what most people can imagine—and also, without doubt, a legacy that endures long after we have left the stage.

Up front, we would do well to consider the costs of a pattern of life that seeks to give its all. When Claus von Stauffenberg died on July 24, 1944, his hopes for a transformed Germany spilled out on the cool stones of a Berlin courtyard. That night, other brave Germans wept and questioned, while the figure who had built his life upon ego and power stood victorious.

But today, we see a fuller picture. While it is nigh impossible to find a parent who will name their child Adolf, virtually every town in Germany has a street named *Stauffenberg Strasse*. This name can be found on streets in many other lands as well, particularly Israel. And the building where Stauffenberg died, once the stronghold of Nazi rule, now holds the German Resistance Memorial Center in honor of Claus von Stauffenberg and others who joined him in pouring out their lives. Now, holding the long view, we see and celebrate the fruit of their struggle.

As you ponder whether you will risk a path like Jesus' in your communication, keep one final thought in mind: The people around you, *all* of them, have deep need of what you now have to offer.

They need you to meet them on their turf and in their terms. They gasp for the pure oxygen of attention. They thirst for refreshing drops of authenticity. They require stories that can rouse them to new truth and weave meaning from the tangled facts of their lives. Their souls cry for more than an echo of the garbled static that surrounds them. They ache to find a friend who truly delights to fill their needs.

You are uniquely equipped to provide these things—not by virtue of towering presence, booming voice, or masterful skills, but in the simple practice of conforming your communication, and your very life, to Jesus' truths.

We now have the tools with which to proceed. The truths we have unearthed are heavy with power and promise. But this is not buried treasure we have discovered; it is a treasure map. Our quest has only begun.

ENDNOTES

INTRODUCTION

1. Yancey, Philip. *The Jesus I Never Knew*, (Zondervan Publishing, 2002) p. 83.

CHAPTER 1: ATTENTIVENESS

1. Bush, Randall. "Not Global Villagers, but Global Voyeurs," *The Christian Century*, September 9-16, 1992, pps. 809-811.

2. Caldwell, Taylor. *The Listener*, (Amereon Ltd., 1960).

3. Reid, Karen. *For My Sister: Reflections on Life, Love, and Sisterhood*, (Andrews McMeel Publishing, 1997) p. 34.

4. Terry, Felber. *Am I Making Myself Clear? Secrets of the World's Greatest Communicators* (Nashville, Thomas Nelson Publishers, 2002) p. 56.

5. Interview in *Rolling Stone* magazine, December 29, 1994, p. 68.

6. Quote from *The Columbia World of Quotations*, (New York: Columbia University Press, 1996); *www.bartleby.com/66/*; *Drawn from Nature*, chapter 3 (1836, revised and repr. 1849).

7. Trogdon, Robert W. *Ernest Hemingway: A Literary Reference* (Caroll & Graf, 2002), p. 174.

8. Postema, Don. *Space for God: Study and Practice of Spirituality and Prayer* (Grand Rapids, Michigan: CRC Publications, 1983) p. 16.

9. Simpson, James B., comp. *Simpson's Contemporary Quotations* (Boston: Houghton Mifflin, 1988); *www.bartleby.com/63/*. Quote drawn from News Summaries 24 Jun 57

10. Pieper, Josef. *Leisure, The Basis of Culture*, Translated by Alexander Dru. (New York: Pantheon Books, a Division of Random House, Inc., 1963.) pp. 40-42.

11. McGinty, Dr. Sarah Myers. *Power Talk: Using Language to Build Authority and Influence* (Warner Books, 2002), p. 66.

12. Dillard, Annie. *The Pilgrim at Tinker Creek*, (New York: Harper Perennial, A division of Harper Collins Publishers, 1974) pp. 34-35.

13. Postema, Don. *Space for God: Study and Practice of Spirituality and Prayer* (Grand Rapids, Michigan: CRC Publications, 1983), p. 20.

14. Albom, Mitch. *Tuesdays With Morrie* (New York: Doubleday, a division of Bantam Doubleday Dell Publishing Group, Inc., 1997), pp. 135-136.

15. Elliot, Elisabeth. *Through the Gates of Splendor* (Tyndale House Publishers, 1986).

CHAPTER 2: SEEKING CONNECTION

1. Lewis, C.S. *Miracles* (New York: Macmillan, 1960.) p. 111.

2. Byrne, Robert. *The 2,458 Best Things Anybody Ever Said* (Fireside, 2002) p. 570.

3. John 1:1, NIV

4. Henry David Thoreau in "Autumnal Tints" (1862), in *The Writings of Henry David Thoreau*, vol. 5. (Houghton Mifflin, 1906), p. 269.

5. Stephen B. Oates. *Woman of Valor: Clara Barton and the Civil War*, (Free Press, 1995); Internet Source: National Park Service, U.S. Department of the Interior, Antietam National Battlefield, Maryland.

6. Quoted in *The Story Factor*, by Annette Simmons (Perseus Publishing. Cambridge, Massachusetts, 2001), p. 27.

7. Simple does not always mean unambiguous. As Dr. Greg Spencer describes, Jesus sometimes spoke with an intentional ambiguity that invited listeners toward further exploration if they truly desired to do so. For example, when Jesus told Nicodemus he would need to be "born again" to enter the kingdom of God, the scholar was puzzled. Jesus' vivid metaphor had been simple—even a child could grasp the basic concept—yet the full meaning was not entirely obvious. Jesus was essentially asking Nicodemus if he wanted to dig deeper. Nicodemus responded as intended, probing further.

8. From Buechner, Frederick. *Listening to Your Life*. Quoted in *The Christian Imagination*, Edited by Leland Ryken. (Colorado Springs, Colorado: Shaw Books, an Imprint of WaterBrook Press, 2002). pg. 56.

9. Chapman, Dr. Gary. *The Five Love Languages: How to Express Heartfelt Commitment to Your Mate*, (Chicago: Northfield Publishing, 1995).

CHAPTER 3: ASKING QUESTIONS

1. Verne, Jules. *Journey to the Center of the Earth*. (Griffith and Farran, 1871).

2. Basler, Roy P. ed. *The Collected Words of Abraham Lincoln*—Volume 1. (Rutgers Univ. Press, New Jersey, 1953), p. 273.

3. From "Crossing the Line," September 3, 2000. Web article on "Carte Blanche Interactive." No author noted. *www.mnet.co.za/CarteBlanche/Display/Display. asp?Id=1432.*

4. Kung, Hans. *On Being a Christian*, Translated by Edward Quinn. (Gordon City, New York: Doubleday & Co., 1976.) p. 286.

CHAPTER 4: AUTHENTICITY

1. Eldredge, John. *Wild at Heart*, (Nashville: Thomas Nelson Publishers, 2001.) p. 52.

2. Coleman, Robert. *The Master Plan of Evangelism* (Grand Rapids, Michigan: Fleming H. Revell, A Division of Baker Book House, 1993) pgs. 41-42.

3. Hammarskjold, Dag. *Markings* (New York: Knopf, 1964), p. 40.

4. Coleridge, Samuel Taylor. *The Rime of the Ancient Mariner*, ed. Paul H. Fry (Boston: Bedford/St. Martins, 1999), p. 34.

5. *New York Times*/CBS Poll taken July 17-19, 1999. *NYT* Poll # 99007B.

6. Vanauken, Sheldon. *A Severe Mercy* (Harper San Francisco, 1987), p. 238.

7. Sozhenitsyn, Alexander. *The Gulag Archipelago* (Perennial, 2002).

8. Buechner, Frederick. *Telling the Truth: The Gospel as Tragedy, Comedy & Fairy Tale* (Harper San Francisco, a Division of Harper Collins Publishers, 1977) p. 26.

9. Ibid., p. 21.

10. Goldsmith, Marshall, Kaye, Beverly, and Shelton, Ken, eds. *Learning Journeys: Top Management Experts Share Hard-Earned Lessons on Becoming Great Mentors and*

Leaders (Davies-Black Publishing, California, 2000), p. 49-50.

11. Coffman, Curt and Gonzales-Molina, Dr. Gabriel. *Follow this Path: How the World's Greatest Organizations Drive Growth by Unleashing Human Potential* (New York: Warner Business Books, 2002).

12. Kraft, Dr. Charles. *Communicating Jesus' Way*, revised edition. (Pasadena: William Carey Library, 1999) pp. 26-27.

13. Willard, Dr. Dallas. *The Divine Conspiracy: Rediscovering Our Hidden Life in God* (Harper San Francisco, 1998.) p. 76.

14. Eldredge, John. *Wild at Heart*, (Nashville: Thomas Nelson Publishers, 2001.) p. 149.

15. *The Columbia World of Quotations* (New York: Columbia University Press, 1996); *www.bartleby.com/66/*. From "Self-Reliance," *Essays, First Series* (1841, repr. 1847).

CHAPTER 5: STORYTELLING

1. Details drawn primarily from Colson, Chuck. *The Body: Being Light in Darkness* (Word Publishing, Dallas, Texas, 1992.) pp. 313-321.

2. Rukeyser, Muriel. *The Speed of Darkness*.

3. Mark 4:34, NIV

4. "Born-again zeal underlies TV's 7th network," by Richard Ostling, Associated Press, *South Coast Advertiser*, October 2, 1998.

5. "The Writer and the Film," *Theater Arts*, Dudley Nichols, October 1943.

6. L'Engle, Madeleine. *Walking on Water* (Harold Shaw Publishers, Wheaton, Illinois, 1980), p. 54.

7. Sandburg, Carl. *Abraham Lincoln: The War Years* (Hardcourt, Brace & Wood, New York), p. 305.

8. Simmons, Annette. *The Story Factor* (Cambridge, Massachusetts: Perseus Publishing, 2001), rear cover.

9. Matthew 13:14, NIV

10. 2 Samuel 12

11. Kraft, Dr. Charles. *Communicating Jesus' Way*, revised edition (Pasadena: William Carey Library, 1999) p. 72.

12. Caracciolo, Annemarie. *Smart Things to Know About Teams* (Capstone Publisher, 2001), p. 212.

13. Haugen, Gary. *Good News About Injustice: A Witness of Courage in a Hurting World* (Downers Grove, IL: Intervarsity Press, 1999), p. 24.

14. "Did God Rescue Those Pennsylvania Miners?" Bill Tammeus, *Akron Beacon Journal*, August 2, 2002.

15. Simmons, Annette. *The Story Factor* (Cambridge, Massachusetts: Perseus Publishing, 2001), p. 111.

CHAPTER SIX: SOLITUDE

1. *Webster's Revised Unabridged Dictionary* 1913, p. 52

2. "Conferences to the Priests of the Mission" by St Vincent de Paul (Conference 207).

3. Luke 5:16, NIV

4. Willard, Dallas. *The Spirit of the Disciplines: Understanding How God Changes Lives* (Harper San Francisco, 1988), p. 164.

5. Sertillanges, A.G., Ryan, Mary (Translator). *The Intellectual Life: Its Spirit, Conditions, Methods* (Catholic University of America, Washington, D.C., 1987).

6. Guiness, Os. *Fit Bodies, Fat Minds* (Baker Book House, 1994).

7. Nouwen, Henri J. M. *The Way of the Heart* (New York: Ballantine Books, 1981.) p. 32.

8. Kundera, Milan. *The Unbearable Lightness of Being* (New York: Harper Row, 1984.) p. 94.

9. Mark 6:31, NIV

10. *The Columbia World of Quotations* (New York: Columbia University Press, 1996). *www.bartleby.com/66/.* From Byron, George Gordon Noel. "Childe Harold's Pilgrimage," cto. 3, st. 90 (1812-1818).

11. Nouwen, Henri J. M. *The Way of the Heart* (New York: Ballantine Books, 1981), p. 13.

12. Popkin, Richard H., ed. *Pascal Selections* (New York: Macmillan, 1989) p. 214.

CHAPTER SEVEN: DEFINING SUCCESS

1. Neider, Charles, ed. *Tolstoy: Tales of Courage and Conflict* (New York: Cooper Square Press, 1999).

2. Hicks, David. *The Emperor's Handbook: A New Edition of Translations* (Scribner, 2002), p. 3.

3. Ecclesiastes 2:11, NIV

4. From the Nirvana Fan Club website, *www.nirvanaclub.com/facts/note.htm.*

5. Lavington, Camille. *You've Only Got Three Seconds* (New York: Doubleday, 1997), pp. xiii-xvi.

6. Merton, Thomas. *The Seven Storey Mountain*, pt. 3, ch. 2 (1948).

7. Maraniss, David. *When Pride Still Mattered: A Life of Vince Lombardi* (New York: Simon & Schuster, 1999), p. 406.

8. Matthew 20:28, NIV

CONCLUSION

1. Winston Churchill, 1940, first speech to House of Commons after becoming Prime Minister.

2. Material drawn primarily from the German Resistance Memorial Center website, *www.gdw-berlin.de/b01/bio/b1-bio-cs1-e.htm.*

3. From his daily national radio address on January 9, 1978 entitled, "Christmas." Contained in *Stories in His Own Hand: The Everyday Wisdom of Ronald Reagan* Edited by Kiron K. Skinner, Annelise Anderson, and Martin Anderson. (New York: The Free Press, 2001), p. 18.

OTHER GENERAL SOURCES

Readings in Classical Rhetoric. Edited by Thomas W. Benson and Michael H. Prosser, (Davis, CA: Hermagoras Press, 1988.)

Bonhoeffer, Dietrich
Quoted in Sander, Oswald; *Spiritual Leadership*, p. 45

Cecil Rhodes story
Am I Making Myself Clear? p.44
Also available elsewhere

The New York Times poll of trust—pg. 7 of *The Story Factor*

When we act unexpectedly, increase impact. (*Communicating Jesus' Way*, p. 26)

George Washington Rebellion Story
Available at *98-99 of Great Communication Secrets of Great Leaders*, p. 98-99.
Available elsewhere, too.
Beethoven story from (Philip Yancey—*More Stories For the Heart*)

Kierkegaard quote: Kierkegaard: Soren Kierkegaard, *The Prayers of Kierkegaard*, Perry LeFebre, ed. (Chicago: University of Chicago, 1956), 147.

Details drawn primarily from an article published in 1974 by the Franciscans of St. Anthony's Guild, Patterson, New Jersey.

Dr. and Mrs. Howard Taylor, *Hudson Taylor's Spiritual Secret*, China Inland Mission, London, 1950.

Bartley's Book of Anecdotes, by A. Clifton/Bernard Fadiman.
"What has struck me is that a truly contemplative and prayerful person seems to have a similar capacity for seeing deeply into reality, the ability to pay attention to what is beneath the surface ..."

Don Postema, *Space for God*, p. 20
Develop strategy for listening. General Marshall having his staff prepare a summary of messages that newly enlisted men were sending home.
From *Great Communication Secrets of Great Leaders*, p. 141

"Today it is very fashionable to talk about the poor. Unfortunately, it is not fashionable to talk with them." —Mother Teresa, *In My Own Words*, p.23

Annie Dillard confirms this thought. "Seeing is of course very much a matter of verbalization. Unless I call my attention to what passes before my eyes, I simply won't see it. It is, as Ruskin says, "not merely unnoticed, but in the full, clear sense of the word, unseen." Dillard, *Pilgrim*, p. 33

Isak Dinesen—"To be a person is to have a story to tell."
Quote on page 1 of *The Story Factor*

[RELEVANTBOOKS]

FOR MORE INFORMATION ABOUT OTHER RELEVANT BOOKS,
check out *www.relevantbooks.com.*